THE ACUPUNCTURE TREATMENT FOR PARALYSIS

THE ACUPUNCTURE TREATMENT FOR PARALYSIS

Compiled by
KONG Yaoqi, REN Xingsheng and LU Shoukang
Translated by
YE Huan and LÜ Guiying

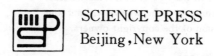

SCIENCE PRESS
Beijing, New York

2 0 0 0

Responsible Editor : HUANG Chengnian

ISBN 7-03-005019-3/R·256
ISBN 1-880132-24-9

PREFACE

Paralysis, a very common disease in clinic, is a disorder which is very difficult to cure. With the progress of the medical science, the diseases that may cause paralysis, such as piliomyelitis and encephalitis B, are becoming less and less. However, on the other hand, some other diseases that may also cause paralysis, such as cerebrovascular accident, are becoming more and more. The high morbidity rate and lowered mortality rate result in a comparative increase of paralysis cases. The incidence of traumatic paraplegia, injury of the peripheral nerves and hysteric hemiplegia is tending to rise. Paralysis often deprives the patients of their working and living capabilities, leaving great sorrow and sufferings to the patients and their families, and heavy burdens to the society. Therefore, it is the unshakable duty for the medical workers to explore the therapeutic methods for various kinds of paralysis and to rid the patients of their diseases.

Treating paralysis with acupuncture has had a history of over 2000 years, during the long period of which very rich experience has been accumulated and rather satisfactory therapeutic effect has been achieved.

On the basis of the study on the experience of the ancient prominent medical figures and clinical practice for many years, the authors have reviewed large quantity of related literatures published over the past 10 years before they finished this book. They have an intimate feeling that acupuncture is indeed a very reliable therapeutic method in the treatment of paralysis. Therefore, it is hoped that this book can be of some benefit to our dear readers.

The authors welcome comments and suggestions.

CONTENTS

CHAPTER ONE
INTRODUCTION

Paralysis refers to complete or incomplete loss of the voluntary movement of a certain part of the body. Clinically, it can be divided into the paralysis of the upper motor neurons, the paralysis of the lower motor neurons and the paralysis caused by disturbance in neuromuscular transmission or muscular diseases.

SECTION I
Paralysis of The Upper Motor Neurons

The paralysis of the upper motor neurons can occur as a result of the injury in the nerve cells or neural axons of the pyramidal tract. This kind of paralysis is usually characterized by the following:

1. Paralysis in voluntary movement but still with reflex. When the limbs of the healthy side move with force or when one is yawning, there will be involuntary movement of the affected limbs.

2. Except in the acute stage of the spinal shock, generally there are increased muscular tonicity and tendon reflex. The paralysis is spastic in nature. The hypertonicity in some muscles is especially apparent. The most common are the flexors of the upper limb and the extensors of the lower limb.

3. With signs of pyramidal tract disturbance, such as the Babinski's sign.

4. There is slight muscular atrophy.

5. Electric stimulation test and myoelectric examination reveal no abnormality.

SECTION II
Paralysis of the Lower Motor Neurons

This disorder is often caused by injuries of the motor cells of the brain stem, or the cells in anterior horn of the spinal cord. This kind of paralysis is characterized by the following:

1. Paralysis in voluntary movement and reflex activities.

2. There will be decreased muscular tonicity, loss or decrease in tendon reflex. The paralysis is flaccid in nature.

3. No signs of pyramidal tract disturbance.

4. There is obvious muscular atrophy.

5. The electric stimulation test shows reaction of degeneration and the myoelectric examination shows denervated changes.

SECTION III
Paralysis Caused by Disturbance in the Neuro-muscular Transmission and Muscular Diseases

Paralysis can be resulted either from the disturbance in the neuromuscular transmission or from the diseases of the skeletal muscles themselves. This kind of paralysis is characterized by the following:

1. Paralysis is flaccid in nature.

2. There are no signs in the pyramidal tract disturbance.

3. The degree of the paralysis varies with the degree of the transmission disturbance and changes of the metabolic myopathy.

4. No reaction of degeneration is found in electric stimulation test. Myopathic changes can be seen in myoelectric examination.

5. There is muscular atrophy in primary myopathy.

According to the sites or limits of paralysis, this disease can be divided into hemiplegia, paraplegia, quadriplegia, monoparesis, paralysis or individual muscle group and infantile cerebral paralysis. As it is one of the most serious and difficult diseases, the therapeutic effect can only be obtained through an exact differentiation and an early treatment.

According to TCM (traditional Chinese medicine) differentiation, paralysis can again be divided into such syndrome types as impairment of fluids in the lung and stomach, deficiency of yin in the liver and the kidney, attack by pathogenic damp and heat, attack by pathogenic cold and damp, qi-deficiency in the spleen, and stomach, deficiency of the kidney-yang, blood stasis in meridians and collaterals, stagnation of the liver-qi and deficiency of blood. In a word, the paralysis in most cases is due to deficiency of the liver and kidney, insufficient qi and blood and attacks by pathogenic factors, such as wind, cold, dampness, heat, phlegm and stasis.

In TCM, acupuncture has long been an effective way in the treatment of paralysis. Working together with various kind of Shu-point treatment methods, such as moxibustion, cupping, ultrared ray radiation, point injection, electrotherapy, catgut embedding and cutting therapy, acupuncture which includes filiform needle needling, scalp needling, ear needling, eye needling and skin needling can play a very important role in strengthening the body resistance, eliminating the pathogenic factors, regulating the qi-blood circulation, removing the obstructions in the meridians and collaterals and tonifying the tendons, muscles and bones. That is why paralysis can be cured with this therapeutic method and patients with this disease can be recovered from this disease satisfactorily.

CHAPTER TWO
THE PRINCIPLES AND MECHANISM OF
ACUPUNCTURE TREATMENT
FOR PARALYSIS

SECTION I
The Principles of Acupuncture
Treatment for Paralysis

1. Searching for the Primary Cause of Disease in Treatment

Although extremities are the common sites of paralysis, yet the pathogenic causes may vary greatly. In clinical practice, we must first of all identify the primary cause of the disease, and then, the treatment is planned accordingly.

When the above principle is used to treat paralysis, we should also determine the superficiality and the origin of the disease according to the changing conditions of every contradiction arising in the course of the disease. Take paraplegia due to cerebral apoplexy as an example. It is clear that the disease is in the brain. The ancient medical book *Plain Questions* narrated "If qi and blood travel simultaneously in the upper part of the body, coma will occur. " Here the location of the disease is also clearly pointed out——in the brain. Therefore, the treatment should be concentrated on "clearing the mind to bring back resuscitation and restoring consciousness"; and the Shu points from the head and the points from the Du Meridian, the Heart Meridian of the Hand-Shaoyin and the Pericardium Meridian of the Hand-Jueyin should be mainly selected. When there is muscular atrophy in the paralysed limb, the spleen is often blamed for, because the spleen has the function to nourish the extremities and their muscles. It is also pointed out in *Plain Questions* that "In the treatment of flaccidity paralysis, take Yangming mainly. " This is the way to deal with the origin, because Yangming Meridian is the sea of the five Zang and six Fu organs, abounding with qi and blood, and is in charge of the tendon. If there is deficiency of the Yangming Meridian, flaccidity paralysis will occur in the limb. Therefore satisfactory therapeutic effect can be obtained only when the key—the Yangming Meridian is grasped in the treatment of flaccidity syndrome.

2. Reinforcing in Deficiency and Reducing in Excess

The entire course of paralysis is actually a process of struggle between the two contradictory aspects—the vital qi and the pathogenic factors. "Excess may result from exuberant pathogenic factors and deficiency may result from exhaustion of the vital essence. " Therefore, "deficiency syndrome should be treated by tonifying method and excess syndrome by purgation and reduction" is another principle in the acupuncture treatment. According to *The Golden Prescriptions*, "Whenever needling is applied, the methods of reinforcing and reducing must be considered first. " The reinforcing method is a manipulation to invigorate the vital qi of the human body, helping the body recover from the weakened state. The reducing method, on the other hand, is a manipulation to remove the pathogenic factors. It can help harmonize the hyperactive body functions. When acupuncture is used to treat paralysis, what we are trying to do is to promote the meridian qi, to regulate the Zang-Fu functions and to balance yin and yang by means of reinforcing or reducing method so that the disease can be cured. Take the treatment of facial paralysis as an example. At the primary stage after the onset, reducing method is generally used. Then uniform reinforcing and reducing method is applied. At the late stage, reinforcing method is performed. This therapeutic procedure is designed according to the fact that at the primary stage, the pathogenic factors are exuberant. During the midstage, the vital energy and the pathogenic factor are almost equal in strength. And at the late stage, the vital energy is insufficient. Meanwhile, the treatment should also be made in accordance with the constitution of the patient. For those with neither deficiency nor excess, uniform reinforcing and reducing should be used; for those with deficiency, reinforcing method should be mainly applied; for those with excess, reducing method should be performed; for those with heat syndrome, the clearing method should mainly be used; and for those with cold syndrome, the warming method should mainly be considered. In addition, the facial paralysis is often caused by the pathogenic wind and cold when the collateral branches in one side of the face is empty. After the attack by the pathogenic factors, the meridian qi is obstructed and the tendon and muscles become poorly nourished. As a result, the loosened muscles deviate to the opposite side of the face. Therefore, in the needling treatment, points from both sides should be taken. Points on the healthy side are needled heavily and those on the affected side needled mildly. This also belongs to "reinforcing in deficiency and reducing in excess".

3. Regulation of Qi and Blood

The major function of acupuncture treatment is to regulate qi and blood. As is pointed out in *Plain Questions*, "Thousands of diseases may arise when there is imbalance between qi and blood." Paralysis, like other diseases, is also caused by the imbalanced qi and blood. Therefore, "to regulate qi and blood" becomes another principle in the treatment of paralysis. Acupuncture has a two-way benign regulatory function. Through its correction of the excess or deficiency of the body, qi and blood are regulated to reach balance so that the disease is cured. Among the syndrome types of paralysis, the most common are qi deficiency, blood stasis, blood deficiency, qi collapse as well as qi stagnation and reversed flow of qi. Therefore, many different techniques or manipulations have to be performed to regulate qi and blood. These include invigoration of qi and vital function, tonification of blood, removal of blood stasis, promotion of the flow of qi and correction of the reversed flow of qi. When there is balanced qi and blood, the muscles and tendons in the four limbs are well nourished. As a result, obstruction in meridians and collaterals are removed and the patient is cured from the paralysis. On the contrary, if we do not consider the proper use of the technology, the disturbance of qi-blood circulation may become even worse and the paralysis become more aggravated.

4. Treating Different Diseases with the Same Therapeutic Method

Different diseases which are alike in pathogenicity can be treated with the same method. This principle is also applicable to the acupuncture treatment of paralysis. Paralysis is a disorder caused by many different diseases such as cerebral hemorrhage, cerebral thrombosis, cerebral embolism, cerebrovascular spasm, subarachnoid hemorrhage, craniocerebral trauma and encephalitis. In the treatment, we can divide it into several syndrome types according to the differentiation regardless of its pathogenic causes, and then treat the disease with the same method. In clinic, the same main points can be selected to treat the same symptoms from different syndrome types. The only difference is that the adjunct points and the needling manipulations should be different. During the recovery stage or the sequelae stage of paralysis, the disease often expresses itself as flaccid or spastic in nature with muscular atrophy and deformity due to imbalanced flexor and extensor. At these stages, the above-mentioned principle is very applicable, i. e. same main points and similar needling manipulation can be used.

5. Treating the Disease According to the Climatic, Seasonal and Individual Conditions

Paralysis can occur in patients of different ages, sexes, constitutions and living habits. Therefore, we have to design the acupuncture treatment according to different individual conditions. Patients with different ages may have different physical functions. Old patients may suffer from deficiency or insufficiency of qi and blood. Most of their diseases belong to deficiency syndromes or "body resistance weakened while pathogenic factors prevailing". Treatment with too much purgation must be avoided, and their vital qi must be invigorated. For the baby patients, their vitality is rather strong, but their Zang-fu organs are very delicate, and their fontanels are often unclosed. In addition, the baby patients are too small to experience and express the needling sensations properly. Therefore in clinic, the point selection, the needling depth, the insertion angles and the needling manipulations should all differ from those used for adult patients. Woman patients have such special conditions as menstruation, pregnancy and delivery. In the treatment, cautions must be taken to the contraindications for point selection. Efforts should also be made to avoid strong stimulation. Even for those with the same age and sex, their individual physical quality is different due to their congenital and acquired constitutions. During the needling, the strength of stimulation should be given accordingly. In addition, for a same patient the manipulations such as reinforcing and reducing and the stimulation induced are also different in different stages of the disease, e. g. the acute stage, the convalescence stage and the stage when there are sequelae.

The paralysis should also be treated according to the climatic and seasonal conditions. For example, the spring and summer are the seasons when the weather grows from warmness to hotness with rising yang qi, and when the human muscles become loose and relaxed. It is very good for moxibustion treatment. In cold weathers when yin is in excess and yang is in deficient, there are usually pain and contracture in the affected limbs. The points and the needling manipulations should be specially selected. In different locality, the climatic conditions are different and the patients may have different physical activities and living habits. In the needling treatment, these factors should also be put into consideration. In addition, attentions should also be

paid to the contraindications of the disease and the diet require-
ment after the needling.

SECTION II
The Mechanism of Acupuncture
Treatment for Paralysis

In the treatment of paralysis, the needling does not always
direct to the etiological factors. Through the action of needling,
it tries to balance yin and yang, to regulate qi and blood, to remove the obstructions in the meridians and collaterals and to
strengthen the body resistance to eliminate the pathogenic factors so that the final goal of curing the disease can be achieved.

There are two basic features we must keep in mind when
TCM is used to treat a disease. One is the "concept of wholism"
and the other is "Bianzheng Lunzhi (planning the treatment according to differentiation)". In the process of needling, whether
we can make full use of the above two features is a key link of a
quicker and better therapeutic effect.

1. The Overall Regulation of the Functions of the Human Body

1) Regulating yin and yang to promote their relative balance
In TCM, it is believed that the occurrence of a disease is always due to the imbalance of yin and yang. Therefore when
acupuncture is applied to treat paralysis, the first thing to do is
to regulate yin and yang and to restore the yin-yang balance.
Take the hemiplegia caused by apoplexy for example. Though it
is caused by the obstruction of blood stasis in the meridians and
collaterals, it can be divided into the following types according to
the concept of wholism—yin deficiency, qi deficiency, blood deficiency, insufficiency of vital qi, etc. If the hemiplegia of qi deficiency or blood stasis type is treated just with the method to promote blood circulation and to remove the blood stasis without
considering the qi deficiency of the disease, the therapeutic effect
can never be obtained. Sometimes it may even aggravate the dis-

ease. "Qi is the commander of blood". "Qi in motion renders blood circulating normally". Qi deficiency often leads to disturbance of the blood circulation. The more severe the blood stasis, the more serious is the imbalance of yin and yang. In addition, "Blood continuously provides nutritions for the functional activities of qi. Qi would get to a deficient state when there is disturbance of the blood circulation due to blood stasis or when much vital qi is consumed for removing the blood stasis. Therefore, the right way to treat hemiplegia of the qi deficiency and blood stasis type is to remove the blood stasis and to supplement qi. Only in this way can the yin-yang balance be restored and satisfactory therapeutic effect be obtained.

2) Strengthening the body resistance and eliminating the pathogenic factors

TCM stresses that the human body is an organic whole. The occurrence and development of a disease is actually a process of struggle between the body resistance and the pathogenic factors. Except for the traumas, the pathogenic cause of paralysis is the insufficient vital qi (body resistance), which can not win over the pathogenic factors. Therefore, in the treatment one can not consider the paralysed limb only. He must try every possible means to strengthen the whole body functions and capability to fight against the disease, and to make the disease transform to the direction of recovery. Meanwhile, one of the reasons to eliminate the pathogenic factors is to prevent the body resistance from being injured. When the vital qi is regained, it can help promote the complete cure of the disease. "Strengthening the body resistance to eliminate the pathogenic factors" is carried out through various kind of needling manipulations, such as reinforcing, reducing and uniform reinforcing and reducing. For example, if a patient with paralysis is found to have muscular atrophy and contracture, we should reinforce the spleen and stomach so that they can absorb nutrients sufficiently and tonify the liver and kidney to strengthen blood and essence, tendons and bones, so that the muscles, meridians and collaterals are properly nourished. The process of curing a paralysis is a long duration. Therefore, it will be very important to reinforce the vital qi of the body from the very beginning.

3) Combination of motion and rest

In the treatment of paralysis, "combination of motion and rest" is regarded as another therapeutic principle. "Motion" refers to both the bodily and mental actions, while "rest" refers to the relative calmness of the both. Both motion and rest are relative. Take the active and passive functional exercise as an example. The active exercise includes both limb movements and mental activities. When the paralysed limb does not move during the needling, some mental activities can be conducted. The patient is able to concentrate his mind to conduct the paralysed limb performing various kind of activities. This can be used as much as possible during the needling treatment. Passive movement includes many traditional ways such as massage and so on. Since the patient can not move his paralysed limb to cooperate with the acupuncture treatment, someone should help the patient to move the diseased limb.

"The combination of motion and rest" can promote qi-blood circulation and is beneficial for the recovery of Zang-fu and limb functions. It can also encourage the patient to set up a confidence to win over the disease and lessen the dependence on drugs. In a word, it can bring the human mechanism into full play. On the other hand, "rest" provides a material basis for "motion". In traditional Chinese medicine, "essence of life", "vitality" and "qi" are three essential factors. "Essence of life" is the essential substances. "Qi" is the material basis to constitute and maintain life activities. "Vitality" is a general term for life process of the human body. "Rest" is actually the calming state of both the body and mentality. It can store the essence of life and the vitality, accumulating and maintaining the basis of the body's movement. Therefore, "rest" can provide the necessary material basis for the "motion".

Therefore, only through the combination of motion and rest

can the mechanism of the human body be brought into full play so as to accelerate the recovery.

2. The Regulation of Qi-Blood Functions in Zang-Fu Organs

TCM holds that in the organism like the human beings, there exists close physiopathological relationships not only between Zang organs, Fu organs, but also between the Zang-fu and other structures, such as skin, muscles, meridians, tendons, bones, nose, mouth, tongue, eyes, ears as well as body essence, qi, blood, saliva, body fluid. Therefore symptoms of paralysis may express themselves as deficiency or excess of the Zang-fu organs or qi and blood. In the treatment, we can cure the disease by regulating the qi-blood and Zang-fu functions. To achieve this, we must first of all analyze the cause (pathogenic factors) and pathogenesis of the disease, identifying which Zang, Fu or extraordinary Fu organ is closely related to the disease and what influence they can insert to the recovery and prognosis. Then differentiated treatment can be applied to the paralysed tissue and organs through regulation of qi-blood function in the Zang-fu organs. For example, muscular atrophy of the paralysed limb is related to the spleen, because it is an important viscus which helps digest food, absorb nutrients and generate qi and blood to support and nourish all the viscera, tissues, and structures of the body. When there is disorder in the spleen, it can not nourish the tendons and muscles. Therefore in the treatment, especially during the recovery stage with sequelae, we must take into account the functions played by this organ and invigorate it by needling and moxibustion. In point selection, the Stomach Meridian of Foot-Yangming and the Spleen Meridian of Foot-Taiyin are often taken. Again in the case of the muscular contracture, numbness, and difficulty in bending and stretching the foot, we often blame the liver, because this organ has the function of dispersing and discharging. It is also in charge of the tendons and muscles and can store blood. If the liver fails to play the functions of dispersing and discharging, such symptoms as depression of the hepatic qi, blood stasis and obstruction of the meridians will be resulted. Tendons are special tissue in charge of moving the joints and muscles. When there is insufficient blood, the tendon can not be nourished properly and many symptoms in the paralysed limb may occur. Therefore in the treatment of paralysis, one of the important ways is to tonify the liver and nourish the blood. Again for example, the kidney is in charge of the bones and it stores the essence of life. The insufficiency of the kidney essence is often one of the reasons for paralysis. Because of the deficiency of the kidney essence, the patient often suffers from weakness of the muscles, tendons and bones of the waist due to poor provision of nutritions to the spinal cord. In the treatment, tonifying the kidney to strengthen the essence of life is of the utmost importance. Therefore the differentiation must be carried out carefully so that the disturbed Zang-fu organs can be properly regulated to a relative balance and the paralysis can be cured satisfactorily.

3. The Regulation of Jingluo

Jingluo (meridians and collaterals) are the passages through which qi and blood circulate, correlate the viscera with the limbs, connect the upper and lower parts with the interior and exterior of the body, and regulate the mechanisms of the various parts of the body. All the tissues and organs of the body including the five Zang and six Fu organs, the four limbs and bones, five sense organs and nine orifices, skin, muscles and tendons are connected into an organic whole by Jingluo.

When Jingluo fail to perform their functions, there will be diseases due to the invasions of the pathogenic factors. When there is a disease of the human body, it can also cause disturbance of the related Jingluo, such as deficiency of the body resistance and excess of the pathogenic factors, disturbance of the blood circulation and imbalanced Jingluo. Therefore, based on the paralysed site and the major symptoms, an analysis on the Jingluo transmission and the Zang-fu organs involved can be used not only as a diagnostic basis, but also as a guide for the needling treatment. Meanwhile, when a disease is found in a certain meridian or Zang-fu organ, points can be selected either from the area which is close to the disease, or from along the meridian. Then proper therapeutic method is applied to regulate the functional activities of Jingluo and qi-blood so as to cure the disease. For example, in the treatment of paralysis, the opposing needling is often applied, that is, reducing is used in the healthy side and reinforcing is used in the affected side. This needling can produce a relative Jingluo balance. Hemiplegia refers to the paralysis of the limbs in one side of the body. Often the three yin meridians and three yang meridians of the hand and foot are involved. As was pointed out in *Corrections on the Errors of Medical Works* by Dr. Wang Qingren, an ancient doctor of Qing Dynasty: "When the primordial qi is insufficient, naturally there will be hollowness of the meridians and collaterals. It is difficult to prevent the qi from moving to one side of the body leading to the empty of qi in the other side. The limbs on that side without qi become paralysed, called "hemiplegia". From this exposition we can see that the affected side belongs to deficiency and the healthy side belongs to excess. Here we can act as what is instructed in *Great Compendium of Acupuncture and Moxibustion*: "In needling paralysis of the hand and foot, we should needle the healthy hand or foot, then the affected hand or foot". Therefore, we should needle the healthy side to reduce the excess and try to balance Jingluo and qi-blood as the first step. Then, the second step is to needle both the healthy side and the affected side, reinforcing the affected side to generate the primordial qi and reducing the healthy side to promote the qi-blood circulation, because at this time there is stagnation of qi and blood in the affected side caused by qi deficiency. Its nature belongs to deficiency complicated with excess. The purpose is to try to produce yin-yang balance. In the third stage, when there is long deficiency of yang-qi and coldness in the meridians of the affected side, the needling is made to promote the flow of yang-qi by warming the meridians and to regulate the qi-blood. The purpose is to produce the relative balance of Jingluo in both sides, including the balance of the three yin meridians and the three yang meridians. In reinforcing the deficiency and reducing the excess by needling, we should also distinguish yin meridian from the yang meridian.

In addition, according to the Jingluo theory and the dual benign regulatory action of the Shu points, the distal-proximal point association can also be used to select the Shu points and stimulating method to treat paralysis, its complications and the sequelae. In the case of traumatic paraplegia, we can mainly use the method of dredging the Du Meridian by needling the Du points in one or two spinous processes above or below the injured level and the Huatuo Jiaji Points. Meanwhile, points as Xuehai, Zusanli, Shenshu, Sanyinjiao etc. can be taken to promote blood circulation and remove the blood stasis, and to strengthen the spleen and stomach. If there is difficulty in bending and stretching both lower limbs, Dachangshu, Zhongliao, Weizhong, Chengshan and Kunlun are added. If both of the lower limbs can not be raised to walk, Huantiao, Yanglingquan, Xuanzhong, Liangqiu, Futu, Zusanli and Xiexi are added, and alternatively electrotherapy is used to dredge the meridians, regulate qi-blood circulation, reinforce the injured meridians and collaterals, reduce the meridians and collaterals with excess and make the Jingluo reach new balance. In this way, symptoms can be improved and the disease is cured.

CHAPTER THREE
CLINICAL THERAPY

SECTION I
Hemiplegia

Etiology and Diagnosis of Hemiplegia

(1) Upper Motor Neurons

    1) Level diagnosis

    a. Cerebrum

In this case, it is often accompanied with hemianesthesia, hemianopsia, aphasia and/or epileptic attacks.

    b. Brain stem

It is marked by crossed hemiplegia, i. e. paralysis of the cranial nerves in the affected side and the paralysis of the limbs in the opposite side.

    c. Cervical medulla

Such symptoms are often noticed as paralysis and bathy-hypesthesia of the upper and lower limbs in the affected side, loss of pain and thermal sensation in the opposite side... etc.

    2) Pathologic diagnosis

    a. Vascular hemiplegia

The onset of the disease is sudden. The patient usually has history of atheroscleorsis, hypertension or cardiovascular and homeopathic diseases.

    b. Traumatic hemiplegia

There is a history of injury of the head or neck.

    c. Neoplastic hemiplegia

The disease develops insidiously and often shows signs of increase of intracranial pressure.

    d. Inflammatory hemiplegia

It is caused by cerebritis or pyencephalus.

e. Others

All the disorders such as congenital and degenerative cerebral diseases or compression of the spinal cord caused by cervical protrusion of intervertebral disc can result in hemiplegia.

(2) Lower Motor Neurons

Occasionally, hemiplegia can also be caused by poliomyelitis or progressive atrophy of the spinal muscles.

Hemiplegia, also called "Pian Ku" in *Internal Classic*, is catalogued in "wind-stroke syndrome" according to the theory of TCM. Acupuncture is found to be effective to the hemiplegia caused by cerebrovascular accident and craniocerebral trauma.

1. Cerebrovascular Accident

This includes cerebral hemorrhage, cerebral thrombosis, cerebral embolism, subarachnoid hemorrhage and cerebrovascular spasm. In TCM, these are totally termed as "wind-stroke syndrome".

Clinical Manifestation

1) Cerebral Hemorrhage

This refers to the profuse hemorrhage inside the brain. About 80% cases occur in cerebral hemisphere, and 20% in brain stem and cerebellum. The major pathogenic causes are hypertension and cerebral arteriosclerosis. According to TCM differentiation, this belongs to "Zang-fu type of wind-stroke syndrome". The main points for diagnosis include:

a. It often occurs in old or middle-aged patients with hypertension or with arteriosclerosis. Before the onset, there is often a sudden rise of blood pressure.

b. The attack starts in most cases, in the daytime due to too much mental stress or emotional agitations.

c. Sudden deep coma may occur in most cases, while progressive coma in some other cases. In a few cases, there may be secondary loss of consciousness.

d. In the early period of disease when the patient is still conscious, there may be sudden headache. In some cases there may be epileptic attacks. About 50% cases may present vomiting. In severe cases, there is gastric hemorrhage with coffee ground vomitus.

e. The patient may have a facial complexion of red or pale and livid colour with irregular breath, slow and forceful pulse, and the blood pressure gets higher than before.

f. The disease is often complicated by paralysis in oneside limb or facial paralysis. In acute stage, there may be disappearance of tendon reflex and superficial reflex.

g. There is increased cerebrospinal pressure with homogeneously bloody cerebrospinal fluid.

h. The CT-scanning may reveal high density hemorrhagic focus in the brain which may involve the ventricular system.

2) Cerebral thrombosis

The most common cause for cerebral thrombosis is cerebral atherosclerosis. According to TCM differentiation, it belongs to Jingluo type of wind-stroke syndrome. The main points for the diagnosis are as follows.

a. This disease is often seen in old patients with a history of cerebral arteriosclerosis and hypertension or with history of diabetes and erythrocytosis.

b. There are apparent prodromal syndromes such as headache, dizziness, hypomnesis, abnormal feelings or weakness of the limbs, and disturbance of speech.

c. The disease often set in when the blood pressure lowers, the blood flows slow and the blood viscosity increases. Therefore the disease is frequently ushered in when the patient is asleep.

d. Generally, the patient is mentally clear. However, some cases in the early period of the disease may experience slight disturbance of consciousness and hemiplegia (central hemiplegia in the limbs of the opposite side, the tongue and the lower part of the face) hemianesthesia and hemianopsia. The paralysis of the limbs is often spastic in nature.

e. There is no obvious change in the body temperature, respiration, pulse rate and blood pressure. The cerebrospinal fluid is normal.

f. CT-scanning shows a low-density infarct lesion which is in line with the distribution of the involved blood vessels — a fan-shaped area with an outward base.

3) Cerebral embolism

The cerebral embolism is often caused by the embolus which is brought by the blood flow to the blood vessels in the brain, leading to ischemia, malacosis and necrosis of the brain tissues. The embolus comes mainly from the heart, especially in the case of rheumatic heart disease with mitral stenosis complicated by auricular fibrillation. The main points for the diagnosis are:

a. This disease is common in young or middle-aged patients with past history and obvious signs of heart disease.

b. Onset of disease abrupt with headache, vomiting and temporary loss of consciousness. When the bigger artery is blocked, there may be coma. Prodromal syndrome is often absent.

c. There exist orientation signs of hemiplegia, hemianesthesia hemianopsia. If primary lesion is in the hemisphere, there is also aphasia. Hemiplegia is most commonly seen. The localized convulsive seizure is more common than that in other cerebral accidents.

d. The cerebrospinal fluid is normal.

e. CT-scanning reveals similar findings as in cerebral thrombosis.

4) Subarachnoid hemorrhage

This is mainly caused by the rupture of cerebral aneurysm or the rupture of abnormal cerebral blood vessels. Both conditions are congenital abnormalities. It can also be caused by the rupture of the fusiform aneurysm formed by atheroscleorsis which covers $5-10\%$ of all acute cerebrovascular diseases. The main points for the diagnosis include:

a. This disease is very common in young or middle-aged and

occasionally in old patients. A past history of intracranial vascular disease or atheroscleorsis may be obtained.

b. The onset is sudden and it may appear at any time when the patient is undertaking a strenuous work or suffers cerebral injury or emotional excitement.

c. The intracranial pressure will increase when there is profuse hemorrhage. There is also transient and slight disturbance of the consciousness. But in most cases, there is no disturbance of the consciousness.

d. The patient may suffer from severe headache, frequent vomiting, stiffness of the neck and obvious signs of meningeal irritation. There may also be epileptic attack if the bleeding stimulates the cerebral cortical motor area.

e. When the blood flows into the brain, parenchyma there, in a few cases, may appear signs of hemiplegia, and hemidysesthesis.

f. There is increased cerebrospinal pressure with homogeneously hemorrhagic cerebrospinal fluid.

g. The CT-scan may reveal a typical high density shadow caused by blood accumulation in the subarachnoid space, cisterna and gyrus.

h. Relapse often occurs immediately after the first onset.

5) Cerebrovascular spasm

According to the recent study, the spasm is due to the increased concentration of calcium ion and decreased hydrogen ion concentration in the hyperplastic smooth muscle cells alongside the atherosclerotic plaque in the cerebral artery. When there is stimulation caused by blood flow, spontaneous spasm may occur. In addition, reflex spasm may also result from the stimulation on the sympathetic nerve when the patient with cervical spondylopathy turns around his head. The cerebrovascular spasm is one of the causes of faint. The main points for the diagnosis are as follows:

a. The onset is sudden with prodromal symptoms such as dizziness, headache, nausea and vomiting.

b. During the attack, the blood pressure rises remarkably. There may be hemiplegia, loss of vision and speech, or even coma and convulsion.

c. The disease course is often very short without any sequelae, but recurrence is frequent.

6) In TCM, this disease is divided into two kinds — Middle Zang-fu and Middle Jingluo. The former is more serious, and can be subdivided into "Blockage" and "Collapse"; the latter is milder.

Middle Zang-fu (apoplexy involving both the solid organs and the hollow organs):

This is the most serious case of apoplexy or wind-stroke syndrome with sudden loss of consciousness, facial paralysis and hemiplegia. If it is complicated by clenching hands, difficulty in urination and defecation, lockjaw, reddish facial complexion, rough breathing due to accumulation of phlegm, thick and greasy tongue fur, and taut and slippery pulse, it belongs to the syndrome of blockage. If the patient also appears closed eyes and open mouth, relaxed hands, snoring sleep, urinary and fecal incontinence, cold limbs, small and indistinct pulse, it belongs to the collapse syndrome.

Middle Jingluo (apoplexy involving the meridians and collaterals):

This is a mild apoplexy with hemiplegia, facial paralysis, stiff tongue and difficulty in swallowing. Most of the symptoms are sequelae after the coma due to wind-stroke syndrome. There were also cases without coma.

Acupuncture Treatment

Hemiplegia may result from cerebrovascular accidents, cerebral hemorrhage, cerebral thrombosis and cerebral embolism. In most cases there will be sequelae of different kind. For the hemiplegia caused by subarachnoid hemorrhage or cerebrovascular spasm, generally there is no sequela. There are some cases of rupture of cerebral aneurysm or rupture of deformed cerebral blood vessels which will have such sequela as hemiplegia. Though the spasm of the cerebral blood vessels has a very brief disease course, it is very common in clinic. Therefore, to the hemiplegia, we can adopt the therapeutic principle of "treating different diseases with the same therapeutic method".

1) Scalp acupuncture

a. Point selection

According to the Standard Nomenclature of Scalp Acupuncture, the points selected for paralysis of the lower limbs include: Dingzhongxian (Middle Line of Vertex), upper 1/5 of the Dingnie Qianxiexian (Anterior Oblique Line of Vertex Temporal) of the healthy side, and Dingpangxian I (Lateral Line 1 of Vertex). For paralysis of the upper limbs include: Dingzhongxian, middle 2/5 of the Dingnie Qianxiexian and Dingpangxian II.

b. Manipulation

After routine sterilization, a No. 30 stainless steel filiform needle 1 to 1.5 cun long is inserted into the scalp rapidly with an angle of 15° between the needle and the scalp. (Note: the hair pores should be avoided.) When the needle enters the galea aponeurotica and a sensation of "grasping of needle" is felt by the fingers, then slowly push the needle, horizontal to the scalp to about 1 cun. Then the manipulation of "qi insertion"or "qi withdrawal"is performed. In performing qi withdrawal, lift the needle swiftly outward with sudden force for three times. Then insert the needle slowly again to about one cun. This can be performed repeatedly. In performing qi insertion, insert the needle inward for three times with sudden force. Each insertion should be no more than 0.1 cun. Then lift the needle to about 1 cun. This manipulation can be also repeated for many times. Generally speaking, in acute stage and in recovery stage, reducing method by qi withdrawal is used, while in sequelae stage, the reinforcing method by qi insertion is used. In the needling, the diseased limb may have sensations of soreness, distension, heaviness, numbness, warmness, coolness, perspiration etc. but some may have not any needling sensation. No matter whether there is the needling sensation, the immediate therapeutic effect, i.e. the arrival of qi (deqi) should be achieved. If there is no deqi, the needle should be manipulated repeatedly until the qi is obtained. After deqi, retain the needle 2 to 24 hours during which the needle can be manipulated for several times. In the acute stage, the treatment is given once daily. 10 treatments are made up of one therapeutic course. In recovery and sequelae stages, the treatment is given once every other day. 5 treatments are made up of one therapeutic course. The spacing between two therapeutic courses is 3 to 5 days or 10 to 20 days respectively.

c. Exercises

During the needling, ask the patient to move the affected limbs to support the treatment . For example , when the upper 1/5 of the Dingjie Qianxiexian or Dingpangxian I is needled, the lower limb should be moved; when the middle 2/5 of the Dingnie Qianxiexian or Dingpangxian II is needled, the upper limb should be exercised. In the limb exercise, ask the patient to concentrate his mind on his affected limbs and to use his conscious activity to guide the active movement of his affected limbs, such as bending the knees, stretching the legs, raising the legs, stamping the foot and bending the elbow, stretching the arm, and raising the hand. Those who can not do active movement, conscious activity can be combined with passive movement. During the time of retaining the needle, the doctor ought to help the patient practise sitting-down and standing-up repeatedly, and then practise walking. For those who could not sit, such exercises as bending the knees, stretching legs, bending the elbow, raising the arms and so on can be carried out in bed. After each needling treatment, the total time of exercise should be no less than 2 hours.

2) Eye acupuncture

a. Point selection

Points around the eyes or in the orbit area can be selected. For paralysis of the lower limbs, Xiajiao on both sides can be taken and for paralysis of the upper limbs, Shangjiao on both sides can be taken. The liver-gallbladder area and the spleen-stomach area can be added according to the conditions of the patient.

b. Manipulation

The patient is in supine position. Press the eyeball with the left hand to tighten the skin of the orbit, then puncture a 0.5 cun filiform needle into the selected point. The needling area should be about 2 mm away from the orbit. The inserted needle can reach the subcutaneous tissue, but no deeper. After the insertion, no manipulation is required. The electrical sensation, the up-and-down feeling sensation, soreness, numbness, or feverish sensation, cooling sensation and comfortable sensation can all be regarded as deqi (the arrival of qi). If no deqi is felt, draw out the needle slightly and reinsert it. If nothing is felt by the patient after insertion, there is no deqi at all. After deqi, retain the needle 5 minutes. When the needle is withdrawn, press the needling point with cotton to prevent from bleeding.

c. Therapeutic course

The needling can be given once a day. 10 treatments are made up of one therapeutic course. The interval between two courses is 3 to 5 days. After two courses, the treatment can be given once every other day.

d. Exercises

During the time of retaining the needle, active exercises or such passive movement as massage can be performed.

3) Acupuncture with filiform needle

Prescription 1

a. Point selection

For paralysis of the lower limbs:

Main points: Huantiao (GB 30), Yanglingquan (GB 34), Zusanli (ST 36), Xuanzhong (GB 39)

Adjunct points: Biguan (ST 31), Futu (LI 18), Fengshi (GB 31), Weiyang (BL 39), Yinlingquan (SP 9), Xiajuxu (ST 39), Sanyinjiao (SP 6), Jiexi (ST 41), Kunlun (BL 60), Taichong (LR 3)

For paralysis of the upper limbs:

Main points: Jianyu (LI 15), Quchi (LI 11), Waiguan (SJ 5), Hegu (LI 4)

Adjunct points: Jingbi (an extraordinary point), Tianquan (PC 2), Zhongzhu (SJ 3), Shousanli (LI 10)

b. Manipulation

The main points must be needled in each treatment and the adjunct points can be needled in turn. In the early stage of hemiplegia, points on the affected side should be needled with the reducing method or with uniform reinforcing and reducing method. For the long-standing cases, the Shu points on the limbs on both sides should be needled with the reinforcing method. During the needling, manoeuver of lifting, thrusting, twirling and rotating is used. After deqi, a stronger stimulation can be given within the patient's tolerance. Needle is retained for 10—20 minutes, during which the needle can be manipulated for several times.

c. Therapeutic course

In the early stage of hemiplegia, the treatment can be given once daily. In the sequelae stage, it is given once every other day. 10 treatments make one therapeutic course. An interval of 5—7 days is needed between two therapeutic courses.

d. Points for attention

When Jingbi is needled, be careful not to injure the apex of the lungs. Deep insertion is not necessary to obtain the required needling sensation.

Prescription 2

a. Point selection

Huatoujiaji points (EX-B 2) 5, 7, 9, 11, and 14. Sometimes Sishencong (EX-HN 1) are added.

b. Manipulation

Patient in prone position or lying laterally. The needle is inserted with an angle of 75° to the skin and the depth is about 1 cun (based on whether the patient is fat or thin). The method of lifting and thrusting for reinforcing and reducing is adopted and the needling sensation should be made to transmit along the costa or the spinal column. The needle is retained for 30 minutes. When Sishencong is needled, oblique insertion can be performed for about 0. 2 cun. Needling can be given once every other day and 10 treatments constitute one therapeutic course. The interval between two courses is one week.

Prescription 3

a. Point selection

Main points: Yamen (DU 15), Fengfu (DU 16)

For paralysis of the upper limbs, Quchi (LI 11), Neiguan (PC 6), Hegu (LI 4), Jiquan (HT 1), Waiguan (SJ 5) and Jianyu (LI 15) are added;

For paralysis of the lower limbs, Fengshi (GB 31), Yanglingquan (GB 34), Sanyinjiao (SP 6), Jiexi (ST 41), Weizhong (BL 40) and Yinbai (SP 1) are added. (The above adjunct points are all taken from the affected side.) On the healthy side, Fengchi (GB 20), Quchi (LI 11), Neiguan (PC 6) and Zusanli (ST 36) are added.

b. Manipulation

The two main points — Yamen and Fengfu can be needled alternatively. With the thumb of the left hand pressing the patient's spinous process of the second cervical vertebra, the doctor should insert a 7. 5 cm-long filiform needle into the point rapidly. When the needle reaches 3. 5 cm deep, the needle is then pushed slowly. Once deqi, withdraw the needle immediately. For the coma patient, the insertion depth is equivalent to 12—14% of the circumference of the neck. In each treatment, 6 to 10 adjunct points can be selected. After deqi, the needles can be connected with a G-6805 stimulator for 20 minutes.

c. Therapeutic course

The treatment is given once daily. 12 to 14 treatments make one therapeutic course, and generally 3—4 courses are needed. Interval between two therapeutic courses is 3 days.

d. Points for attention

When Yamen and Fengfu are needled, observe the patient carefully and as soon as deqi is elicited, stop the needle getting in more. The regression equation between X (circumference of the neck of the patient, and Y (the insertion depth for Yamen and Fengfu) is

$$Y \text{ (cm)} = 2.6475 \pm 0.0778 \text{ X (Fengfu)}$$
$$Y \text{ (cm)} = 2.7183 \pm 0.07 \text{ X (Yamen)}$$

Generally, the depth should be 12% to 14% of the cervical circumference.

Prescription 4

a. Point selection

Main points: Nejguan (PC 6), Renzhong (DU 26), Sanyinjiao (SP 6)

Adjunct points: Jiquan (HT 1), Chize (LU 5), Weizhong (BL 40), Hegu (LI 4)

b. Manipulation

First acupuncture Neiguan bilaterally for 1—1.5 cun in depth, using lifting-thrusting manoeuver for 1 minute. Then acupuncture the Renzhong pointing obliquely to nasal septum for 0.5 cun in depth. Manipulate the needle with bird-peck like reducing method until tear appears. Then Sanyinjiao is needled obliquely backward with an angle of 45° to the skin and 1—1.5 cun in depth. Lifting-thrusting reinforcing method can be used until 3 jerks are found in the lower limb. For point Jiquan, perpendicular insertion for 1 to 1.5 cun can be performed. Lifting and thrusting reducing method is used until 3 jerks are found in the upper limb. For point Chize, perpendicular insertion for 0.8 to 1 cun with lifting-thrusting reducing method can also be performed until there are 3 jerks found on the upper limb. For point Weizhong, patient lies in supine position with the leg raised. Perpendicular insertion is made 0.5 to 1 cun in depth. Lifting-thrusting reducing method can be performed until 3 jerks are found in the lower limbs. For those whose fingers are not able to

extend or flex, penetration needling throughout Hegu and Sanjian (LI 3) can be performed. Lifting-thrusting reducing method
can also be used.

c. Therapeutic course

Two treatments can be given daily. 10 treatments constitute
one therapeutic course.

Prescription 5

a. Point selection

Needle penetration from Jianyu (LI 15) to Binao (LI 14),
Quchi (LI 11) to Shaohai (HT 3), Sidu (SJ 9) to Bizhong;
Yanglingquan (GB 34) to Yinlingquan (SP 9), Kunlun (BL 60)
to Taixi (KI 3)

Needle penetration from Quchi (LI 11) to Zhigou (SJ 6),
Hegu (LI 4) to Houxi (SI 3); Liangqiu (ST 34) to Futu (ST
32), Xuehai (SP 10) to Qimen (LR 14), Zusanli (ST 36) to
Chengshan (BL 57), Sanyinjiao (SP 6) to Juegu (GB 39)

Adjunct points can be selected according to the symptoms of
the patients.

b. Manipulation

The above-mentioned two groups of points can be used alternatively. A No. 28 filiform needle of 2.5 to 5 cun long is
adopted. After deqi, perform twirling, together with lifting-
thrusting for 1 to 3 minutes. After a spacing of 5 minutes, the
same manipulation can be performed once more. Then repeat the
whole performance for 3 to 4 times. The stimulation should be
tolerable for the patient. When a strong sensation of soreness,
distension or heaviness is felt by the patient, the needling can be
stopped.

c. Therapeutic course

A therapeutic course consists of 6 treatments weekly.

d. Points for attention

The direction of needling must be correct so as to ensure the
needle can reach the required points. Lifting-thrusting with large
amplitude should be avoided because the needling is rather deep.

Move of the needle tip should also be avoided lest injury or hematoma result. The intensity of twirling should be increased gradually. The depth of the insertion should be varied with various conditions of the patient.

Prescription 6

a. Point selection

For paralysis of the upper limb: Needling throughout Dazhui (DU 14) and Zhiyang (DU 9)

Adjunct points: Needling throughout Jianyu (LI 15) and Quchi (LI 11) or Waiguan (SJ 5) and Quchi (LI 11), or Hegu (LI 4) and Houxi (ST 3)

For paralysis of the lower limb: Needling throughout Zhiyang (DU 9) and Jinsuo (DU 8) and Mingmen (DU 4) to Yangguan

Adjunct points: Huantiao (GB 30) and Kunlun (BL 60)

Baxie (EX-UE 9), penetration from Zusanli (ST 36) to Juegu (GB 39), from Yanglingquan (GB 34) to Kunlun (BL 60), Qiuxu (GB 40), from Yinlingquan (SP 9) to Sanyinjiao (SP 6) can be added according to the symptoms of the patient.

b. Manipulation

The filiform needle of 2 to 3 cun in length and 0. 5—2 mm. in diameter is used. The patient can take a suitable position during the neeling. When the points on the shoulders are needled, the needling sensation should transfer to the fingers. When the points on the wrist are needled, the needling sensation would transmit to the chest and shoulder. When Huantiao is needled, the needling sensation transmit down to the toes. When Kunlun is needled, the needling sensation transmit up to the shoulder and back.

c. Therapeutic course

Treatment is given once daily. 10 treatments constitute one therapeutic course.

4) Ear acupuncture

a. Point selection

Subcortex, Brain stem, Heart, Liver, Spleen, Kidney, Sanjiao and Wrist, Elbow, Shoulder, Hip, Knee, Ankle and other ear points related to paralysis.

b. Manipulation

Rapid twirling needle insertion is undertaken with moderate stimulation. 1 minute later, there would be auricular congestion. The skin turns reddish and the temperature of ear rises. The patient feels feverish in his ear, face and head. Within 5 minutes there will be a feeling of warmness and relax. Usually a retaining of needle for 30 minutes is needed.

c. Therapeutic course

The needling can be given once every other day. 15 treatments constitute one therapeutic course.

5) Point injection

Prescription 1

a. Point selection

Baihui (DU 20), Shangxing (DU 23)

b. Manipulation

1 ml. of Chuanxiongqin (Ligustrazine) is injected into the point. A horizontal penetrating needling is performed from Baihui to Shangxing or vice versa. When deqi is elicited with lifting-thrusting method, patient would appreciate sensation of soreness, numbness, heaviness, and distension. If there is no blood on drawing back the syringe, the drug can be injected to the point area.

c. Therapeutic course

The point injection is given once daily. The two points are used in turn. 30 injections constitute one therapeutic course.

Prescription 2

a. Point selection

Jianzhongshu (LI 15), Neiguan (PC 6), Fengshi (GB 31), Chengshan (GB 57)

Quchi (Li 11), Waiguan (SJ 5), Yinlingquan (SP 9), Kunlun (BL 60)

The two groups of points can be used alternatively.

b. Manipulation

After deqi, if there is no blood on drawing back the syringe, 0. 5 ml. of Danshen (Radix Salviae Miltiorrhizae) injection can be injected into each point.

c. Therapeutic course

The injection is given once daily or every other day. 15 injections constitute one therapeutic course.

Prescription 3

a. Point selection

Fengchi (on the affected side)

b. Manipulation

In the early stage of the disease, 1. 5 ml. of 5% γ-Aminobutyric Acid or 10—15 mg. adenosine triphosphate can be injected into the point. In late stage of the disease, 100 mg. Vit. B$_1$ plus 50 mg. Nicotinamide can be used for the injection.

c. Therapeutic course

The injection can be given once everyday or once every other day. A therapeutic course consists of 10 injections.

d. Point for attention

Once deqi is elicited, no further advancement of the needle is necessary.

6) Skin acupuncture (Skin needle therapy)

a. Point selection

Shenshu (BL 23), Ganshu (BL 18), Baliao (eight extra points), Jiaji (EX-B 2), Quchi (LI 11), Taiyuan (LU 9), Yanglingquan (GB 34), Fengshi (GB 31), Xuanzhong (GB 38), Dadun (LR 1)

b. Manipulation

Tap the points on the back and paralysed limbs from up downwards and from the center part to the peripheral parts. Light to moderate stimulation is performed until local redness with no bleeding.

c. Therapeutic course

The treatment is given once everyday. Ten treatments constitute one therapeutic course.

7) Catgut implantation

a. Point selection

Shousanli (LI 10), Quchi (LI 11), Zusanli (ST 36), Yanglingquan (GB 34), Sanyinjiao (SP 6)

b. Manipulation

In each treatment, 1 to 3 points are selected, sterilization and local anaesthesia are carried on as usual. A segment of catgut of 2 to 3 cun long is threaded into the lumen of the needle. And insert the needle with its bevel facing upwards subcutaneously to the assigned point where the catgut is further pushed into the subcutaneous space. Then turn the bevel of the needle downwards and advance the needle further. With one hand on the skin to fit the catgut embedded subcutaneously with cotton of tincture iodine and covered with gauze.

c. Therapeutic course

This therapy can be given once a month, and is indicated for patients with sequelae.

d. Points for attention

Too deep local anaesthesia should be avoided, otherwise it would decrease the therapeutic effect. Analgesics may be used when there is pain postoperatively. Bacteriocidal agents or antibiotics may be given when it is necessary. Some people allergic to foreign body as catgut may receive anti-allergic drugs as Chlorpheniramine maleate or Prednisone.

8) Moxibustion

Prescription 1

a. Point selection

Tianchuang (ST 16), Baihui (DU 20)

b. Manipulation

Moxibustion with moxa sticks. First of all, Tianchuang on the healthy side, then Baihui is moxibustioned. When the patient has a warm-hot sensation, it means that the temperature is suitable. This treatment can be given 1 to 2 times a day and each session can last 15 minutes. 30 days' treatment is made up of one therapeutic course. A rest for 3 to 5 days is required between two therapeutic courses.

Prescription 2

a. Point selection

Daihui (DU 20), Faji (hairline anterior to the ear), Jianjing (GB 21), Fengchi (GB 20), Quchi (LI 11), Zusanli (ST 36), Xuanzhong (GB 39), Kunlun (BL 60)

b. Manipulation

In each treatment, 4 to 5 points are selected. 3 to 5 moxa sticks are required for each point. The treatment can be given once everyday or once every other day. 10 treatments constitute one therapeutic course.

Prescription 3

a. Point selection

Baihui (DU 20), Sishengcong (EX-HN 1), Fengchi (GB 20, bilateral), Yanglingquan (GB 34, bilateral); Zhengyin (GB 17); Baihui (DU 20), Tinghui (GB 2), Dicang (ST 4), Qubin (GB 7), Fengchi (GB 20), Dazhui (DU 14), Jianyu (LI 15), Quchi (LI 11), Fengshi (GB 31), Zusanli (ST 36), Juegu (GB 39)

The above 3 groups are known as "12 points for windstroke syndrome" (apoplexy).

b. Manipulation

Using a red-hot pin to replace moxibustion. Holding a pin with forceps and burning it to red-hot over the alcohol lamp, the operator inserts the pin vertically into the point about 1 cm. in depth. In each treatment this kind of point-needling can be repeated for 3 times. For hemiplegia acupuncture the point Zhengying on the opposite side. Smoke the point with moxa for 90 to 120 minutes in each treatment. Two treatments can be given everyday. These points can be moxibustioned with moxa sticks in turn. Sometimes, direct moxibustion on the point is also applicable.

9) Laser irradiation of points

a. Point selection

For paralysis of the upper limb:

Jianyu (LI 15), Quchi (LI 11), Waiguan (SJ 5), Hegu (LI 4)

For paralysis of the lower limb:

Huantiao (GB 30), Yanglingquan (GB 34), Weizhong (GB 40), Zusanli (ST 36), or Jianyu (Li 15), Sidu (SJ 9), Biguan (ST 31), Zusanli, Sanjian (LI 3)

b. Manipulation

A He-Ne laser machine with a power of 10 mw is used. The diameter of the light spot is about 2 mm and the distance between the machine and the skin is about 50 cm. In each treatment, 4 points can be irradiated and each irradiation can last for 4 to 8 minutes.

c. Therapeutic course

The treatment is given once every other day. 10 treatments constitute one therapeutic course. A spacing of one week is required between 2 therapeutic courses.

10) Microwave acupuncture

After routine sterilization, a needle of No. 28 or 30 is inserted into the point. After deqi, connect a DBJ-I microwave acupuncture machine to the handle of the needle. Adjust the output power so that the patient feels no pain. Each treatment can last for 15—20 minutes. The treatment is given once every other day. A therapeutic course consists of 10 treatments.

Therapeutic Effect

1) The author treated 192 cases of hemiplegia due to windstroke syndrome, out of whom 171 cases were caused by cerebral thrombosis, 14 cases by cerebral hemorrhage, 4 cases by cerebral embolism and 3 cases by subarachnoid hemorrhage. The

therapeutic results are as follow: 146 cases were cured (76.04% of the total), 34 cases had remarkable therapeutic effect (17.71%), 10 cases had certain effect (5.21%) and 2 cases with no effect (1.04%). The total effective rate was 98.96%. (Journal of Jiangsu Traditional Chinese Medicine 1989; 7:10)

2) Dr. Peng Jingshan et al. reported the therapeutic results of 242 cases of hemiplegia treated with eye acupuncture. The cure rate was 23.14%, remarkable improvement rate 38.43%, effective rate 35.95% and no improvement 2.48%. The over-all effective rate was 97.52%. It was claimed that the patient with cerebral thrombosis especially within the duration of 3 months have the best prognosis and excellent therapeutic results. (Journal of Chinese Acupuncture 1988; 8:10)

3) Dr. Wang Yigang et al. studied 251 cases of hemiplegia treated by acupuncture with traditional filiform needle and revealed an over-all effective rate of 96.8%. The curative rate for those with a disease duration less than 3 months was 41.5% and that with a duration over 4 months was 21.3%. The prognosis for cerebral thrombosis was better than that for cerebral hemorrhage. The difference of their prognosis is significant. (Journal of Chinese Acupuncture 1987; 7:6)

The author had also treated many sequelae of hemiplegia. The over-all effective rate was over 95%.

Dr. He Shuhui had treated 40 cases of wind-stroke syndrome with the acupuncture on Huatoujiaji (EX-B 2) 5, 7, 9, 11 and 14. The results showed that 32 cases (80%) were cured. 5 cases (12.5%) obtained remarkable therapeutic effect. 3 cases (7.5%) were improved with an over-all effective rate of 100%. (Journal of Beijing TCM College 1983; 2)

4) Acupuncture on Fengfu (DU 16) and Yamen (DU 15) are mainly indicated for hemiplegia caused by cerebral hemorrhage. Starting from the acute stage, acupuncture the main points. When the disease became stable, the adjunct points should be added. According to a clinical observation on 38 cases by Dr. Li Dingming, 29 cases (76.3%) had restored the myody-

namia of the upper limb to degree IV; 35 cases (92. 1%) had restored the myodynamia of the lower limb to degree IV. Compared with the control group (those who did not receive acupuncture on the two points mentioned above), the results were 40. 6% and 62. 5% respectively, P value<0. 01.

5) Acupuncture on Neiguan (PC 6), Renzhong (DU 26) and Sanyinjiao (SP 6) is a method to treat hemiplegia caused by the wind-stroke syndrome. This is known as "the method of restoring mind and inducing resuscitation". A clinical observation on 279 cases was made by Dr. Zhai Yide. The average days of treatment was 53 days. The curative rate was 61% and the over-all effective rate was 98%. (Journal of Chinese Acupuncture 1988; 5:8)

Dr. Shi Xuemin had treated 54 cases of cerebral hemorrhage with 28 cases (51. 85%) cured, 15 cases (27. 8%) with remarkable effect, 11 cases (20. 35%) improved. The over-all effective rate was 100%. (Journal of Chinese Acupuncture 1984; 5 : 4)

6) After treating the sequelae caused by wind-stroke syndrome with ear acupuncture in adjunct with scalp and body needling, Dr. Zhang Zhanjun held that the combined acupuncture method could get better therapeutic result on the hypermyotonia, especially on the functional disturbance of the elbow, wrist and ankle of the affected limb than that treated in one way with the scalp or body acupuncture. He had treated 165 cases, among whom 55 cases were cured, 70 cases obtained remarkable effect, 35 cases were improved and 5 cases were with no effect. The over-all effective rate was 97%. (Journal of Chinese Acupuncture 1988; 11:8)

7) Moxibustion has been found to have positive therapeutic effect on hemiplegia. Dr. Zhang Dengbu had treated 33 cases with warm moxibustion on Tianchuang and Baihui. As a result, 13 cases (39. 4%) were cured, 13 cases (39. 4%) greatly improved, 6 cases (18. 2%) were improved, only 1 case (3. 0%) was of no effect. The over-all effective rate was 97%. When 30 cases were chosen at random for rheoencephalogram before and

after the treatment for study, it revealed that the blood flow in the brain had been greatly improved after the moxibustion with statistical significance. (Journal of Shandong TCM 1987; 6)

8) Laser irradiation can improve the cerebral blood circulation and lower the viscosity of the blood. Dr. Song Tiecheng had treated 60 cases of this disease with laser irradiation on the points. The results showed that 14 cases (23.4%) were cured, 25 cases (41.6%) were remarkably improved, 18 cases (30%) were improved, and 3 cases (5%) were of no effect. The overall effective rate was 95%. (Journal of Shanxi TCM 1987; 5:3)

Discussion

1) Cerebrovascular accident is a disease with high incidence, high mortality and high disability. The acupuncture in the treatment of hemiplegia has become one of the major contemporary subjects in research.

There are different methods in the application of acupuncture for hemiplegia. In the course of treatment, one single, or several therapeutic methods in combination can be adopted. Generally the therapeutic result is rather satisfactory. The author considers the combined use of several methods may offer better results and they can be used alternatively.

2) In the past, some physicians believed that "the patient with acute cerebral hemorrhage must have a complete bed rest for 4 to 6 weeks and that all kind of stimulations should be avoided. Otherwise, there will be hemorrhage again and the disease, more aggravated. (Xiao Zhenxiang et al: Cerebrovascular Diseases, People's Medical Publishing House 1979; p. 280)

However, the modern study reveals that the chances for recurrent hemorrhage are few after the first attack. A 20 years follow-up study on 1500 cases of cerebral hemorrhage caused by hypertension reveals only 30 cases suffering from rehemorrhage. Besides, the rehemorrhage does not occur in the early stage of the disease but occurs mostly in the period between 3 months to two years. There was a case of earliest rehemorrhage seen two months after the first hemorrhage, and autopsy confirms that the rehemorrhage never happens in the original site, because the scar formed by the first hemorrhage has played a protective role to the fragile small blood vessels. Meanwhile, there was lowered blood flow with lower pressure in these area and it is not easy to have rehemorrhage. (Sui Bangsen: Diseases of Civilized Society Which Threaten the Human Life, Xinhua Publishing House 1988; p. 166)

After a careful study, Dr. Li Dingming pointed out that needling Fengfu (DU 16) and Yamen (DU 15) immediately after the cerebral hemorrhage did no harm to the patient, but rather it could help shorten the disease course and raise the therapeutic effect. It was shown by experiments that needling within 10 days after the onset, the cure rate and the basically cure rate were 39.4% and 21.05% respectively. In total, it was 60.52%. When the needling conducted within the 11th to 30th days, no cured case was found and the basically cure rate was 50%. Therefore, it is very essential to needle Yamen and Fengfu as soon as possible so as to shorten the therapeutic course and raise the effect. (Journal of Chinese Acupuncture 1987; 7:3)

From his study, Dr. Shi Xuemin and his colleagues also considered that early needling is a key point in the treatment of the disease. The proper time of the treatment is closely related to the therapeutic effect. According to the study, the cure rates for those treated within 2 weeks, within 4 weeks and over 4 weeks were 68.4%, 47% and 38.9% respectively. The author thinks that the earlier the acupuncture for the cerebral thrombosis, the better the therapeutic results. The same is true for cerebral hemorrhage. When the life sign becomes stable, acupuncture therapy should begin together with functional exercises. The earliest time for the author to start the treatment for cerebral hemorrhage is 7 days after the onset.

3) Comparing the therapeutic effects of acupuncture between cerebral hemorrhage and cerebral embolism, some authors revealed that patients with cerebral hemorrhage could have a

quicker recovery, and fewer sequelae. The hemorrhage and hematoma could be absorbed slowly or even disappeared. This has been confirmed by the CT-scanning, and is also in accordance with the clinical improvement. (Shi Xuemin: Journal of Chinese Acupuncture 1984; 4:5)

4) With acupuncture therapy, too strong stimulation should be avoided when the blood pressure of the patient exceeds 26/15.6 kpa (200/120 mm Hg). Burns should be prevented when moxibustion is applied on unconscious patients.

5) Prophylactic measures might be taken for hypertensive patients against the cerebrovascular accidents, Quchi (LI 11), Yintang (EX-HN 3) etc. can be needled in turn and ear acupuncture can also be performed.

6) In patients with cerebrovascular accidents besides facial paralysis, there are also other associated symptoms such as aphasia, hemianesthesia, and dysphagia and so on. These can be treated by needling corresponding points according to the differentiation.

7) For the scalp acupuncture, there exist different schools, such as Jiao Shunfa's method, Fang Yunhe's method, Tang Songyan's method and Zhang Mingjiu's method, all of which have good therapeutic effect on hemiplegia.

8) The eye acupuncture can only be applied to those patients with clear minds, without symptoms of the Middle Zang-fu organs, without disfunction of the muscles or the limbs and with the myodynamia of degree 0 to 3. For those patients with deformation of the joints or limbs, the eye acupuncture should be avoided.

2. Traumatic Hemiplegia

Severe injuries on the head or neck can cause hemiplegia, resulting in sequelae of different kind.

Clinical Manifestations

1) Most head or neck injuries are due to direct violence,

such as hitting, pricking, or striking by hard objects. When falling from a high place, the force can also be transmitted to the head or neck through the spinal column. Similarly, the inertia force due to emergency braking of a car can also cause injuries of the head and neck.

2) If the skull fracture involves the functional area of the brain, it can cause paralysis of the corresponding part of the body. In the area where fracture occurs, besides injury of the scalp, bone pitting can also be touched.

3) When the blood vessels in the meninges are injured due to skull fracture, or when there is hemorrhage of the brain tissues, there may be such signs as platycoria of the same side, uncompleted paralysis of the limbs on the opposite side, the appearance of pathological reflex, increased blood pressure, slow but forceful pulse and slow but deep breathing.

4) The ultrasonic examination of the head may indicate that the midline deviates to one side. If the displacement is more than 0.4 cm, it indicates presence of intracranial hematoma.

5) Cerebral angiography can indicate the location of hematoma.

6) CT-scanning can reveal the skull fracture and site of intracranial hemorrhage.

Acupuncture Treatment

The principle of treatment for cerebrovascular accidents can be taken as a reference. If the scalp acupuncture can not be used on the injured side, it can be applied to the other side, and satisfactory therapeutic effect can also be achieved. For the treatment of hemiplegia caused by the injuries on the neck, please refer to the treatment on paraplegia.

3. Sporadic Encephalitis

Encephalitis is a kind of inflammatory change in brain parenchyma by the invasion of the pathogenic micro-organism. It can be divided into (a) viral encephalitis which mainly involves the nerve cells, (b) non-viral encephalitis which involves all the nerve tissues and (c) encephalitis of unknown etiology. Sporadic encephalitis belongs to the last category.

In recent years, there are more and more reports on sporadic encephalitis, a disease of uncertain causes and without unified criteria of diagnosis. It is likely, in most cases, to be a demyelinating disease which may result in hemiplegia of different degrees or paraplegia on both sides.

Clinical Manifestation

1) Usually the onset is acute or subacute. Those with acute onset have their symptoms to the peak in a few days, while those with subacute onset have their peak symptoms about 10 days to 2 months later. This disease is with no seasonal or endemic nature.

2) About half of the sporadic encephalitis cases show prodromal symptoms such as aversion to cold, fever, headache, general malaise, sniffy or running nose, cough, abdominal pain, diarrhea, nausea and vomiting. In a few cases, there are conjunctivitis, herpes labialis, myalgia and so on.

3) In about half cases, the initial symptom is psychic or mental disturbance which includes sluggishness, hypoplasia, absence of mind, apathetic disturbance of association, lowered ability of understanding and judgement, disturbance at orientation, calculation and memory; failure to carry out the original job, answer irrelevant to the questions, childish behavior and idleness. Slowly the patient may have urinary incontinence and he can not manage his life by himself. On the other hand, some patients may have hyperphasia, excitement, then illusion, delusion and restlessness.

4) The disturbance of consciousness can develop from lethargy and mental confusion to coma.

5) The epileptic attack, in most cases is a grand mal.

6) Very often, there are pyramidal signs in one side or in both sides, resulting in hemiplegia or paraplegia of both sides,

and pathological reflex of both sides. Part of the cases may have palmomental reflex, sucking reflex and symptoms of pseudobulbar paralysis.

7) There are also injuries of the cranial nerves such as paralysis of the oculomotor nerve, the abducent nerve, facial nerve and hypoglossal nerve, nystagmus, and dysphagia. There may also be symptoms of the brain stem, such as bulbar paralysis, crossed paralysis or contralateral sensory disturbance. There are also ataxia, aphasia, sensory disturbance and signs of meningeal irritation.

8) Perspiration or even profuse sweating. There is also high fever of central origin.

9) There may be such symptoms of increased intracranial pressure as headache, vomiting and papilloedema and even cerebral hernia.

10) Peripheral white cell count increases to 10.000/mm^3 in some cases.

11) Generally, the cerebrospinal fluid is clear. The pressure, number of cells, biochemical indexes of the cerebrospinal fluid are all normal in over half of the cases. In a few cases, the pressure may become higher and the number of white cells may increase within a limit of 100/mm^3. Most of them are lymphocytes.

12) EEG findings in 80—90% cases are abnormal. Most of them belong to diffuse abnormality and changes at the temple and frontal areas, including polymorphic high-voltage slow waves, mainly δ waves. The EEG examination can help the early diagnosis of the disease.

13) The ultrasonic detection can find the displacement of the mesal wave in some cases.

14) CT-examination can detect the diffuse lesion with rough margin and lowered density, most of which are located in the white matter.

Acupuncture Treatment

In the convalescence of this disease, acupuncture therapy can be instituted. The therapeutic method is the same to that for the hemiplegia caused by cerebrovascular accidents. After the treatment, most cases can be cured or obtain satisfactory therapeutic results. Besides, it can also be treated with the method of point injection.

1) Point selection

Jianyu (LI 15), Shousanli (LI 10), Sidu (SJ 9) and Neiguan (PC 6) in the upper limb

Futu (LI 18), Jianxi (3 cun above the patella), Zusanli (ST 36) and Sanyinjiao (SP 6) in the lower limb

For those with neck flaccid, Tianzhu (BL 10) and Dazhui (DU 14) are added; for those who can not stand or sit, Shenshu (BL 23) and others are added.

2) Manipulation

Point injection with Scopolamine Butylbromide, 0.01—0.05 mg/kg body weight daily.

3) Therapeutic course

The treatment is given once daily. 30 treatments makes one therapeutic course. A spacing of 7 to 10 days can be arranged between two courses, if necessary.

4) Points for attention

Scopolamine possesses certain adverse reactions such as blurred vision, delirium, weight loss, vomiting, poor appetite, restlessness, skin rashes, urinary frequency or retention, uncontrollable motions of the extremities, joint pain, headache, and pale face. These side actions occur in about 39.4% cases and will subside with decrease of dosage.

5) Therapeutic effect

Dr. Zhang Xiouhui reported the clinical experience on 46 cases of sporadic encephalitis treated with point injection of Scopolamine. He achieved cure in 5 cases (10.8%), remarkable effect in 12 cases (26.1%), improvement in 27 cases (58.7%)

and no effect in 2 cases (4.3%). The over-all effective rate was 95.7%. A follow-up of 3 years found only 2 relapse cases.

6) Discussion

Modern studies consider that paralysis and muscular atrophy are closely related to nerve injuries, ischemia and the disturbance in acetylcholine metabolism. The effective component of Scopolamine is scopoletin. It has the effect to regulate the function of the blood vessels, to dredge the microcirculation and to provide the nerve and muscle with essential nutritions. It can also help repair the injured spinal nerves, inhibit the feedback mechanism of nerve and adjust the balance of the acetylcholine. Meanwhile, it can also promote the synergistic action between the drug and the point. (Journal of TCM 1988; 2:29)

4. Post-hemiplegic Syndrome

Hemiplegia, no matter what the causes are, may lead to certain kind of sequelae. This may result from the severe disease conditions, delayed treatment or lack of physical exercises. To cure the sequelae and restore the health, several ways of acupuncture treatment are introduced as follows.

Ankylosis

1) Needling with filiform needles

a. Point selection

Points in Yin Meridians and muscle tendons around the joints

For ankylosis and pain in the scapular region: Quyuan (SI 13), Tianzong (SI 11)

For ankylosis of the elbow joints: Yingshang (three transverse fingers width above olecranon process and one transverses finger width to the ulnar side), Tianjin (SJ 10), Zhouliao (LI 12)

For ankylosis of the finger joints: needle penetration from Hegu (LI 4) to Laogong (PC 8), Sanjian (LI 3)

For ankylosis of the knee joints: Xiyangguan (GB 33),

Ququan (LR 8)

For ankylosis of the toe joints: Bafeng (EX-LE 10)

b. Manipulation

When Yinshang is needled, the needle is inserted obliquely upward for 1.5 cun deep. Lifting and twirling with large amplitude are required to induce stronger stimulation. For the rest points, uniform reinforcing and reducing method should be employed. The needle is retained for 20 minutes.

c. Therapeutic course

One treatment every other day. 10 treatments makes one therapeutic course.

2) Electroacupuncture therapy

a. Point selection

Same as those in needling with filiform needles.

b. Manipulation

After deqi, connect the needle with a G-6805 electric stimulater for 15 to 20 minutes. The continuous wave should be used and the stimulation should be strong enough to make the patient's joint relax.

c. Therapeutic course

The treatment is given once every other day. A therapeutic course consists of 10 treatments.

3) Scalp acupuncture

a. Point selection

For the ankylosis of wrist, elbow, and shoulder joints: Middle 2/5 section of Dingnie Qianxiexian is selected.

For the ankylosis of angle, knee and hip joints: upper 1/5 section of Dingnie Qianxiexian is selected.

The section is divided into 3 equal parts and 3 needles are inserted from up downwards.

b. Manipulation

The method of "qi withdrawal" is performed, and retain the needle for 2 to 24 hours.

c. Exercises

During the needling and retaining of needles, active or passive movement of the joints concerned should be carried out.

4) Ear acupuncture

a. Point selection

Commonly used points: Shoulder, Elbow, Wrist, Finger, Hip, Knee, Angle, Toe, Clavicle and Liver

b. Manipulation

A 0.5 cun filiform needle should be used with stimulation of moderate intensity, and the needle is retained for 20 minutes.

c. Therapeutic course

The treatment is given once every other day. 10 treatments constitute one therapeutic course.

Pain of the Limbs

1) Acupuncture with filiform needle

a. Point selection

Points around the affected area are often selected.

b. Manipulation

Reducing method by lifting, thrusting and twirling is applied, and the needle is retained for 20 to 30 minutes.

c. Therapeutic course

The treatment is given once every other day. A therapeutic course consists of 10 treatments.

2) Electroacupuncture therapy

a. Point selection

Same as those with filiform needle.

b. Manipulation

After deqi, connect the needle with a G-6805 electric stimulater for 15 to 20 minutes.

c. Therapeutic course

The treatment is given once every other day. 10 treatments constitute one therapeutic course.

3) Warm-needle acupuncture

a. Point selection

Same as those with filiform needle.

b. Manipulation

After deqi, put a moxa stick on the needle handle and light it. Or moxibustion can be applied on the needling site after the needle is withdrawn until the local skin becomes reddish.

c. Therapeutic course

The treatment is given once everyday. 10 treatments constitute one therapeutic course.

4) Ear acupuncture

a. Point selection

Subcortex, Shenmen, Adrenal Gland and the pain-corresponding sensitive points, such as Shoulder, Elbow, Wrist, Finger, Hip, Knee, Ankle, Toe, Cervical Vertebrae, Thoracic Vertebrae, and Lumbosacral Vertebrae.

b. Manipulation

Puncture with a 0.5 cun filiform needle to induce strong stimulation. Retain the needle for 20 minutes. The needle can also be connected with a G-6805 electric stimulator for 15 to 20 minutes. The continuous wave is applied.

c. Therapeutic course

The treatment is given once everyday or once every other day. 10 treatments constitute one therapeutic course.

5) Point irradiation with ultra-red ray

a. Point selection

Points surrounding the pain area

b. Manipulation

For the pain in the muscle-rich area like the limbs, elbow and knee, the short-wave ultra-red ray can be applied. For the Shu points in the limb ends, the long-wave ultra-red ray should be used. Each treatment lasts 20 to 40 minutes.

c. Therapeutic course

One or two treatments everyday. One therapeutic course consists of 10 to 20 treatments.

Weakness in Lifting the Knees

1) Scalp acupuncture

a. Point selection

Upper 1/5 of Dingnie Qianxiexian or Dingpangxian I and Dingzhongxian

b. Manipulation

Apply "qi withdrawal" when the needle enters the lower layer of the galea aponeurotica. Retain the needle for 2 to 24 hours.

c. Therapeutic course

The treatment is given once every other day. 10 treatments constitute one therapeutic course.

d. Exercises

During needling and retaining of needle, active or passive exercises such as lifting the knees should be practiced. Exercise of this kind should be no less than 2 to 4 hours everyday.

2) Ear acupuncture

a. Point selection

Knee, Hip

b. Manipulation

Induce moderate to strong stimulation with a 0.5 cun filiform needle. Retain the needle for 30 minutes.

c. Therapeutic course

Treatment is given once every other day. Proper exercise should be conducted to support the treatment.

3) Acupuncture with filiform needle

a. Point selection

Xuehai (SP 10), Liangqiu (ST 34), Yinshi (ST 33), Futu (ET 32)

b. Manipulation

Apply uniform reinforcing and reducing method. Retain the needle for 15 to 20 minutes after deqi.

c. Therapeutic course

Treatment is given once every other day. 10 treatments constitute one therapeutic course.

4) Electrotherapy

a. Point selection

Same as above.

b. Manipulation

After deqi, connect the needle with a G-6805 electric stimulator for 15 minutes. The continuous wave should be used.

c. Therapeutic course

Treatment is given once every other day. 10 treatments constitute one therapeutic course.

Foot Drop

1) Filiform needle needling

a. Point selection

Zuqi (1. 5 cun above the middle point on the line joining the medial and the lateral malleolus, in the anterior aspect of the leg and the lateral margin of the tibia).

b. Manipulation

Puncture rapidly with a No. 26 filiform needle of 1. 5 cun long. Lifting, thrusting and large amplitude twirling and rotating should be performed to induce strong stimulation. Withdraw the needle after deqi.

c. Therapeutic course

One treatment everyday. A therapeutic course consists of 10 treatments.

2) Electrotherapy

a. Point selection

Yanglingquan (GB 34), Yinlingquan (SP 9), Xiajuxu (ST 39), Qiuxu (GB 40), Shangqiu (SP 5), Jiexi (ST 41)

Take 2 to 4 points in each treatment.

b. Manipulation

After deqi, connect the needle with a G-6805 electric stimulator for 15 minutes. The continuous wave is used.

c. Therapeutic course

Treatment is given once every other day. 10 treatments constitute one therapeutic course.

3) Ear acupuncture

a. Point selection

Ankle, Heel

b. Manipulation

Induce strong stimulation with filiform needle. Retain the needle for 30 minutes or connect it with a G-6805 electric stimulator for 15 minutes.

c. Therapeutic course

Treatment is given once every other day. 10 treatments constitute one therapeutic course.

Difficulty in Flexion and Extension of the Fingers

1) Filiform needle needling

a. Point selection

Jianshi (PC 5), Neiguan (PC 6), Shenmen (HT 7), Waiguan (SJ 5), from Hegu (LI 4) to Sanjian (SI 3) or from Hegu to Laogong (PC 8), Baxie (EX-UE 9)

b. Manipulation

Take 2 to 3 points from Baxie in each treatment and twirling is performed 100 times. No needle retaining is needed. For all the rest points, reducing by lifting and thrusting should be applied.

c. Therapeutic course

Treatment is given once every other day. 10 treatments constitute one therapeutic course.

2) Scalp acupuncture

a. Point selection

Upper part of the 3 equal parts in the Middle 2/5 Dingnie Qianxiexian.

b. Manipulation

Apply "qi withdrawal" when the needle enters the lower layer of the galea aponeurotica. Retain the needle for 2 to 24 hours.

c. Therapeutic course

Treatment is given once every other day. 10 treatments constitute one therapeutic course.

d. Exercises

Both active and passive exercise should be taken to support

the treatment.

3) Ear acupuncture

a. Point selection

Fingers

b. Manipulation

Strong stimulation is induced by filiform needle needling. Retain the needle for 20 minutes or perform auricular-plaster therapy with seeds of vaccaria segetalis.

c. Therapeutic course

The ear acupuncture is given once everyday or once every other day. If the auricular-plaster therapy is applied, press the point with hands for 3 to 4 times everyday. This therapy can be given once a week.

4) Point irradiation with ultra-red ray

a. Point selection

Shu points in the fingers

b. Manipulation

Irradiate the fingers of the affected side with ultra-red ray for 30 minutes.

c. Therapeutic coures

One or two treatments a day. Treatments of 7—10 day duration make one therapeutic course.

Grasp Weakness

1) Filiform needle needling

a. Point selection

Jinjin (EX-HN 12), Yuye (EX-HN 13), Haiquan (EX-HN 11) (central point of the frenulum of tongue)

b. Manipulation

A No. 28 filiform needle of 1 cun is used to prick Jinjin and Yuye which are located under the tongue, there slight bleeding may occur. Then prick 1 to 2 needles around these two points. At last, prick Haiquan. During pricking direct the needle tip pointing to the root of tongue.

c. Therapeutic course

One treatment every other day.

2) Scalp acupuncture

a. Point selection

The upper part of the 3 equal parts on the Middle 2/5 of Dingnie Qianxiexian.

b. Manipulation

"Qi withdrawal" should be performed when the needle enters the lower layer of galea aponeurotica. Retain the needle for 2 to 24 hours. During needle retention, manipulate the needle 3 to 5 times.

c. Therapeutic course

Treatment is given once every other day. 10 treatments constitute one therapeutic course.

d. Exercises

During needling or needle retention, instruct the patient to perform flexion-extension of the fingers and hand-grasping. Other rehabilitating instruments such as grip exerciser can also be used.

Swelling of Limbs

1) Filiform needle needling

a. Point selection

Main points: Jianyu (LI 15), Chize (LU 5), Waiguan (SJ 5), Baxie (EX-UE 9), Biguan (ST 31), Yinlingquan (SP 9), Fenglong (ST 40), Sanyinjiao (SP 6)

Adjunct points: Zhongwan (RN 12), Shuifen (RN 9)

b. Manipulation

Reducing method with lifting-thrusting and twirling-rotating for points on the limbs; moxibustion after needling for points on the abdomen is added.

c. Therapeutic course

One treatment is given every other day. A therapeutic course consists of 10 treatments.

Talipes Varus and Talipes Valgus

1) Filiform needle needling

a. Point selection

For talipes varus: (a) Zusanli (ST 36) through Juegu (GB 39) Yanglingquan (GB 34) through Kunlun (BL 60), supported by Qiuxu (GB 40); (b) Zuneifan (talipes varus-correction point — 1 cun lateral to the point Chengshan)

For talipes valgus: (a) From Yinlingquan (SP 9) to Sanyinjiao (SP 6); (b) Zhaohai (KI 6); (c) Zuwaifan (talipes valgus-correcting point — 1 cun medial to the point Chengshan)

b. Manipulation

For penetrating needling, a stainless steel needle is used. When the needle tip enters the subcutaneous part, twirl the needle along the meridian for the penetration. When Shenmai (BL 62) or Zhaohai are needled, reinforcing by lifting-thrusting and twirling the needle should be performed. For both talipes varus and valgus, uniform reinforcing and reducing maneuver is applied.

c. Therapeutic course

One treatment is given every other day. A therapeutic course consists of 10 treatments.

2) Scalp acupuncture

a. Point selection

Upper 1/5 of Dingnie Qianxiexian

b. Manipulation

Perform "qi withdrawal" and retain the needle for 2 to 24 hours.

c. Therapeutic course

One treatment is given every other day. A therapeutic course consists of 10 treatments.

d. Exercises

During needling or retaining meedle, ask the patient to exercise the foot in an attempt to correct the deformity. When in bed, the affected foot should be kept in the functional position by a wooden fixer. When walking, the patient should be ordered to use his muscles to regain the muscle strength with weight-carrying exercise and progressive resistive exercises. Patient with talipes varus should do abduction or outward rotation.

Shoulder Failure to Raise

1) Filiform needle needling
a. Point selection
(a) 0.5 cun lateral to the 6th cervical vertebra; (b) Jianyu (LI 15), Jianliao (SJ 14); (c) Tianzong (SI 11), Jianliao, Naohui (SJ 13), Binao (LI 14); (d) Jiquan (HT 1); (e) Zhongping (the crossing point of 1 cun below Zusanli and 2 cun above Shangjuxu)
b. Manipulation
Any group from the above can be selected. After inserting the needle at 0.5 cun lateral to the 6th cervical vertebra, puncture obliquely to the spinous process. When there is a numbness distension feeling after the uniform reinforcing and reducing, the patient can be able to raise the arm. When points in group (b) and group (d) are needled, the points on the affected side should be taken, Insert the needle perpendicularly and reducing method by lifting, thrusting, twirling and rotating is applied. For group (c), the points should also be taken from the affected side. Reinforcing by lifting, thrusting, twirling and rotating is applied. Zhongping of the healthy side should be needled in a standing position, if possible. For those who can not stand, take a sitting or supine position. After deqi, order the patient to move the shoulder as much as possible. Usually a No. 28 filiform of 2 to 3 cun long can be used.
c. Therapeutic course
One treatment is given every other day. A therapeutic course consists of 10 treatments.
2) Scalp acupuncture
a. Point selection
Lower part of the 3 equal parts in Middle 2/5 Dingnie

Qianxiexian, Dingpangxian II. For shoulder pain, Dingnie Houxiexian is added.

b. Manipulation

"Qi withdrawal" is applied. Retain the needle for 2 to 24 hours. Manipulate the needle several times during the retaining of needle.

c. Therapeutic course

One treatment is given every other day. A therapeutic course consists of 10 treatments.

d. Exercises

During needling and retaining of needle, order the patient to perform active or passive shoulder joint movement.

3) Ear acupuncture

a. Point selection

Shoulder, Clavicle

b. Manipulation

Apply strong stimulation with a 0. 5 cun filiform needle. Retain the needle for 30 minutes or connect the needle with a G-6805 electric stimulator for 15 minutes.

c. Therapeutic course

One treatment is given every other day. A therapeutic course consists of 10 treatments.

Weakness of the Lower Limbs

1) Filiform needle needling

a. Point selection

For weakness in thigh abduction: Huatoujiaji (EX-B 2) L4-5, Juliao (GB 29), Tiaoyao (2 cun below the summit of iliac crest posteriorly)

For weakness in thigh adduction: Jimai (LR 12), Yinlian (LR 11), Xuehai (SP 10), Qimen (LR 14)

For weakness in knee bending: Chengfu (BL 36), Yinmen (BL 37), Weizhong (BL 40), Huantiao (GB 30)

For weakness in knee extension: Chongmen (SP 12), Biguan (ST 31), Futu (ST 32), Siqiang (4. 5 cun above the middle point of the superior margin of patella).

b. Manipulation

Perform uniform reinforcing and reducing method.

c. Therapeutic course

One treatment is given every other day. A therapeutic course consists of 10 treatments.

2) Needle warming through moxibustion

a. Point selection

(a) Taixi (KI 3), Sanyinjiao (SP 6); (b) Zhongwan (RN 12), Guanyuan (RN 4), Zusanli (ST 36)

b. Manipulation

Reinforcing with lifting, thrusting, twirling and rotating for the points in group (a). After deqi, a moxa stick of 2 cm long can be added on the needle. Slight stimulation should be applied on the points in group (b). After deqi by needling, moxibustion is applied with the above-mentioned method.

3) Moxibustion

a. Point selection

Shenshu (BL 23), Pishu (BL 20), Guanyuan (RN 4), Zusanli (ST 36)

b. Manipulation

Moxibustion with moxa sticks until the local area becomes reddish. For those with general malaise, Baihui (DU 20) should also be moxibustioned.

c. Therapeutic course

Two treatments everyday, 10 days' treatments make one therapeutic course.

4) Scalp acupuncture

a. Point selection

Upper 1/5 of Dingnie qianxiexian, Dingpangxian I

b. Manipulation

When the needle enters the galea aponeurotica, apply reinforcing method with qi entering. Insert the needle swiftly forward with force for 3 times, and each insertion is no more than 0. 1 to 0. 2 cun deep. Retain the needle for 2 to 24 hours.

c. Therapeutic course
Same as above.

d. Exercises

Such functional exercises as standing and walking should be practiced during needling or retaining of needle.

Sourness and Weakness of Waist

1) Scalp acupuncture

a. Point selection

Zhenshang Zhengzhongxian, Zhenshang Pangxian

b. Manipulation

Perform "qi withdrawal". Retain the needle for 2 to 24 hours, during which the needle should be manipulated for several times.

c. Therapeutic course

One treatment is given every other day. A therapeutic course consists of 10 treatments.

d. Exercises

Practice bending, raising and rotating the waist during needling and retaining of needle.

2) Filiform needle needling

a. Point selection

Shenshu (BL 23), Zusanli (ST 36), Taixi (KI 3), Sanyin-jiao (SP 6)

b. Manipulation

When the first two points are needled , strong stimulation should be induced. For Taixi and Sanyinjiao, reinforcing method with lifting, thrusting, twirling and rotating should be applied.

c. Therapeutic course

One treatment is given every other day. A therapeutic course consists of 10 treatments.

3) Ear acupuncture

a. Point selection

Lumbosacral Vertebrae. Kidney, Gallbladder

b. Manipulation

Moderate to strong stimulation should be induced with filiform needle. Retain the needle for 15 to 20 minutes.

c. Therapeutic course

One treatment everyday or every other day.

4) Cupping

a. Point selection

Shenshu (BL 23), Dachangshu (BL 25), region of lumbar
vertebrae

b. Manipulation

Apply cupping on the above-mentioned points or area for 5
to 10 minutes.

c. Therapeutic course

Same as ear acupuncture.

5) Point irradiation therapy with ultra-red ray

a. Point selection

Lumbar vertebrae area and the Shu points aside

b. Manipulation

Irradiate the local part with ultra-red ray for 30 minutes.

c. Therapeutic course

Same as ear acupuncture.

Muscular Atrophy

1) Filiform needle needling

a. Point selection

Zhongwan (RN 12), Qihai (RN 6), Sanyinjiao (SP 6), Zusanli (ST 36), Xuehai (SP 10) are taken as main points.

Jianyu (LI 10), Quchi (LI 11), Waiguan (SJ 5), Hegu (LI
4), Huantiao (GB 30), Fengshi (GB 31), and Yanglingquan
(GB 34) can be taken selectively as the adjunct points according
to the disease condition of the patient.

b. Manipulation

In each treatment, 2 to 3 main points and 2 to 3 adjunct
points can be needled. The points can be made into groups and
needled in turn. Reinforcing method is applied by lifting, thrusting, twirling and rotating. Retain the needle for 30 minutes.

c. Therapeutic course

One treatment is given every other day. A therapeutic course consists of 10 treatments.

2) Electric therapy

a. Point selection

Same as above.

b. Manipulation

Generally, 2 main points and 2 adjunct points are taken in one treatment. The points can be needled in turn. After deqi, connect the needle with a G-6805 electric stimulator for 15 minutes. The continuous wave should be used.

c. Therapeutic course

One treatment is given every other day. A therapeutic course consists of 10 treatments.

3) Scalp acupuncture

a. Point selection

Epangxian II (both sides), Dingnie Qianxiexian (opposite side of the focus), Dingpangxian I and II (opposite side of the focus).

b. Manipulation

Qi entering method is applied. Retain the needle for 2 to 24 hours, during which the needle can be manipulated several times.

c. Therapeutic course

One treatment is given every other day. A therapeutic course consists of 10 treatments.

d. Exercises

Limb exercises and muscle massage can be practiced. Try to produce strong stimulation with pushing or squeezing the muscles.

4) Ear acupuncture

a. Point selection

Spleen, Endocrine, Kidney, Liver, Subcortex

b. Manipulation

Puncture the points with filiform needles, twirl the needles once every 5 minutes. Retain the needles for 30 minutes.

c. Therapeutic course

Same as above.

5) Moxibustion

a. Point selection

Shu points on the area corresponding to the atrophic muscles.

b. Manipulation

Moxibustion with moxa sticks. Each treatment can last 10 minutes until the local skin becomes reddish.

c. Therapeutic course

Same as above.

Hemianesthesia

1) Filiform needle needling

a. Point selection

Zhongwan (RN 12), Qihai (RN 6), Houxi (SI 3), Shenmai (BL 62)

b. Manipulation

Perform reinforcing method by lifting, thrusting, twirling and rotating. Moxibustion can also be applied for 10 to 20 minutes after the needling.

c. Therapeutic course

One treatment is given every other day. 10 treatments make one therapeutic course.

2) Scalp acupuncture

a. Point selection

For numbness of the lower limb: Upper 1/5 of the Dingnie Houxiexian of the healthy side

For numbness of the upper limb: Middle 2/5 of the Dingnie Houxiexian of the healthy side

b. Manipulation

Reducing with the method of qi withdrawal is applied. Retain the needle for 2 to 24 hours, during which the needle can be manipulated several times.

c. Therapeutic course

One treatment is given every other day. A therapeutic course consists of 10 treatments.

d. Exercises

Massage the affected part to support the therapeutic effect.

Discussion

1) The treatment of hemiplegia sequelae is actually "mending the fold after escaping of sheep". The rehabilitation measures should begin even from the acute stage of the disease. For example, one of the early symptoms of hemiplegia is joint pain. It is generally considered that this symptom is caused by disturbance of the blood circulation, changes of the nourishment and uneven tension of muscles around the joint. In the case of cerebral accident, the thalamus-syndrome may interfere the vegetative nerve functions, resulting in hemiplegia. Pain of the limbs can be prevented by the following measures: Proper nutrition to the joints and its surrounding tissues, and adjusting the muscle tension in the early stage of disease.

2) Acupuncture is effective to hemiplegia sequelae. It can support the vital essence of the body and reinforce the deficiency. It can also expel the pathogenic wind, activate blood circulation, relax the tendons and nourish the joints. Satisfactory therapeutic effect can often be obtained when certain extraordinary points are needled. One of the examples is the treatment of weakness in grasping by pricking the points under the tongue. Dr. Jin Hong had made an observation on the treatment of 15 patients with weakness in grasping. The age of the patients ranged from 47 to 68 and the duration of disease ranged from 6 days to 4 months. The test for grasping power 5 and 30 minutes before and after the treatment showed that 3 cases were cured (The grasping strength increased by 8 kg. reaching 15 kg). 3 cases were remarkably improved (The grasping strength increased by 4 kg. reaching 5 kg). 8 cases were effective with some improvement and one case was with no effect. The total effective rate

was 93. 33%. (Journal of Jiangsu TCM 1987; 12:8)

Dr. Zheng Yunfei treated hemiplegia sequelae with big needle therapy. The total effective rate was 93.3%. For the mild cases, usually 1 to 2 therapeutic courses could obtain cure. For serious cases, only 2 to 3 therapeutic courses are needed. (Journal of Chinese Acupuncture 1988; 4:8)

3) The therapeutic effect can be improved if some other traditional therapies can be applied to support the needling. These include massage therapy, oral herbal medicine, functional exercises, Qigong therapy, etc.

SECTION II
Paraplegia

Paraplegia refers to the paralysis of limbs caused by nerve block after injury of the spinal cord. It consists of paralysis of both lower limbs and the paralysis of the four limbs caused by injury of cervical spinal cord. Besides injury, other causes of disease mainly are: acute or chronic inflammation of the spinal cord, spinal compression and degeneration.

Paraplegia is divided into two kinds — complete paraplegia and incomplete paraplegia. The complete paraplegia is caused by a transverse lesion, characterized by total disappearance of sensory, reflex, and vegetative nervous system function below the injured level. The incomplete paralysis refers to a lesion in certain part of the spinal cord, not completely transversing the whole plane. This incomplete lesion in the spinal cord may block partly nervous transmission such as by compression, severe contusion or concussion of the spinal cord.

In TCM paraplegia belongs to "flaccidity syndrome", and is caused by damage to the Du Meridian. The Du Meridian possesses function governing all the yang meridians, and the confluence of all the yang meridians of the hand and foot into the Du Meridian. When damage of the Du Meridian occurs, the blocked circulation of qi and blood will cause qi-blood stagnancy in the three hand or foot meridians. As a result, there will be numbness, loss of sensations, failure to move, etc. of the limbs. Furthermore, there may also be imbalance of yin and yang, such as disturbance of urinary and defecation functions.

1. Clinical Manifestations

In clinic, the diagnosis of spinal injury is mainly based on physical examination, that is according to the examination on the functions of the spinal cord. Those with complete impairment of the spinal transmission function found in clinical examination belong to transverse lesion or complete paraplegia, though pathologically the spinal cord is not severed completely.

2. Acupuncture Treatment

1) Filiform needle needling

Prescription 1

a. Point selection

Main points: Nine Points for needling on cross-section (One point on the spinous process of the injured level, one point on the L5 spinous process and one point on the midpoint between these two processes, and the six Huatuojiaji points on both sides of the above three points. These are collectively termed as Nine Points for needling on cross-section.)

Adjunct points: If there is disturbance in urination and defecation, following points can be added: Baliao (Eight-Liao) points, Tianshu (ST 25), Qihai (RN 6), Zhongji (RN 3), 0.5 cun by the side of Zhongji and Sanyinjiao (SP 6)

b. Manipulation

Needling the points of Du Meridian: Press the skin around the point with left index and middle fingers and insert the needle perpendicularly with the right hand. Slow and even lifting and thrusting is performed. Generally the insertion depth is about 1.5 cun to 2.5 cun according to the conditions of the patient. When an elastic resistance is felt by the operator, the needle can be pushed deeper. However, when there is a sudden, hollow breaking — through sensation, that is, when there is a tingling sensation in the lower limbs or perineum of the patient, the insertion must be stopped.

Needling Huatoujiaji points: Insert the needle with the above method, and the needling sensation may radiate to both sides or may appear as tightness sensation in the body cavity of the corresponding part. Also the needling sensation may refer to the upper or lower limbs. Insert the needle 1 to 1. 5 cun to the direction of the intervertebral foramen. During the needling, the method of lifting, thrusting, twirling and rotating can be applied.

In needling Tianshu, the needling sensation is required to transmit to the groin, while in needling points of Ren Meridian, the needling sensation is required to transmit to the pudendum. For injury of the spinal cord, mild stimulation is advisable and for the injury of cauda equina, moderate stimulation should be performed with uniform reinforcing and reducing.

c. Therapeutic course

One treatment is given everyday or every other day. 10 treatments constitute one therapeutic course. A spacing of 5 to 7 days is required between two courses.

Prescription 2

a. Point selection

Main points: 1 to 2 Du points of the spinous process respectively above and below the injury level, or 1 to 2 Huatoujiaji points in between 2 spinous processes respectively above and below the injury level.

Adjunct points: Guanyuan (RN 4), Zhongji (RN 3), Tianshu (RN 22), Zhibian (BL 54), Yinmen (BL 37), Weizhong (BL 40), Kunlun (BL 60); Biguan (ST 31), Futu (LI 18), Chongyang (ST 42), Zusanli (ST 36); Yanglingquan (GB 34), Juegu (GB 39)

b. Manipulation

All the points are needled perpendicularly. The insertion depth for the main points should be 1.5 to 2.5 cun. When Du points are needled, the same method as mentioned above should be applied. Attention should be paid to slow and even lifting and thrusting. If there is a sudden breaking-through feeling by the hand or there is an electric-shock feeling felt by the patient in the perineum or the lower limbs, the insertion should be stopped immediately so as not to injure the spinal cord. Reinforcing or reducing should be performed with lifting, thrusting and twirling for the adjunct points. Zhongji and Guanyuan can be used alternately. Before needling, the patient should void completely to get rid of the bladder not being injured and the needling depth is about 1 to 1.5 cun.

c. Therapeutic course

Same as above.

Prescription 3

a. Point selection

Shenshu (BL 23), Dachangshu (BL 25), Ciliao (BL 32), Huantiao (GB 30), Zhibian (BL 54); Guanyuan (RN 4), Zhongji (RN 3), Qichong (ST 30), Zusanli (ST 36), Yanglingquan (GB 34), Taixi (KI 3)

b. Manipulation

First needle the Shu points on the back with strong stimulation by the method of twirling, lifting and thrusting. When Huantiao and zhibian are needled, the patient should have the sensation of soreness and numbness, or flash-like sensation referring to the third and small toes. Perform intermuscular needling on Dachangshu and the insertion is made to reach the deep part of the sacrospinal muscle. First make the needling sensation radiate through the Foot-Taiyang Meridian to the toes, then warm the needle with 3 to 5 moxa-cones, and make the warm-heat go through the Shu point into the deep part. When points on the abdomen and the feet are needled, strong stimulation should be performed by lifting, thrusting, twirling and rotating. Then moxibustion is performed as mentioned above. Retain the needle for 15 minutes.

c. Therapeutic course

Two treatments are given every week. 20 treatments constitute one therapeutic course.

Prescription 4

a. Point selection

(a) Points of Du Meridian: Renzhong (DU 26), Dazhui (DU 14), Taodao (DU 13), Shenzhu (DU 12), Zhiyang (DU 9), Jizhong (DU 6), Xuanshu (DU 5), Yaoyangguan (DU 3), supported by Baihui (DU 20), Shendao (DU 11), Jinsuo (DU 8), Mingmen (DU 4)

(b) Huatuojiaji points: Points corresponding to the Du points

(c) Points of the Bladder Meridian of Foot-Taiyang: Dazhu (BL 11), Back Shu points of various Zang-fu organs, Geshu (BL 17)

(d) Points of the Stomach Meridian of Foot-Yangming: Liangmen (ST 21), Tianshu (ST 25), Shuidao (ST 38), Guilai (ST 29), Biguan (ST 31), Yinshi (ST 33), Zusanli (ST 36), Shangjuxu (ST 37), Xiajuxu (ST 39) Liangqiu (ST 34), Jiexi (ST 41)

(e) Points of the Gallbladder Meridian of Foot-Shaoyang: Jingmen (GB 25), Wushu (GB 27), Weidao (GB 28), Huantiao (GB 30), Fengshi (GB 20), Yanglingquan (GB 34), Xuanzhong (GB 39), Qiuxu (GB 40), and Zulinqi (GB 41) supported by Taichong (LR 3)

(f) Points of Ren Meridian and 3 Foot Yin Meridians are taken as adjunct point selectively: Chengjiang (RN 24), Zhongwan (RN 12), Jianli (RN 11), Shuifen (RN 9), Qihai (RN 6), Guanyuan (RN 4), Zhongji (RN 3), Zhangmen (LR 13), Sanyinjiao (SP 6), Diji (SP 8), Xuehai (SP 10), Yongquan (KI 1)

b. Manipulation

Points of the Du Meridian and the Huatuojiaji points are

needled with the above-mentioned method. When the points of the abdomen are needled, the needling sensation refers to the pudendum and when the points on the lower limbs are needled, the needling sensation refers to the toes. On all above points reinforcing method is used and the patient would feel heaviness and warmness sensations. No retaining of needle is needed. The above points from various meridians can be used selectively, or according to the differentiation.

c. Therapeutic course

The treatment is given once everyday or once every other day. 10 to 12 treatments are make one therapeutic course. A spacing of 7 days is needed between two courses.

2) Scalp acupuncture

a. Point selection

Dingzhongxian, Upper 1/5 of Dingnie Qianxiexian (lower limb), Middle 2/5 of Dingnie Qianxiexian (upper limb) bilaterally.

b. Manipulation

Method of "qi withdrawal" should be used. First needle Dingzhongxian. Insert the needle from Qiandin (DU 21) rapidly to Baihui (DU 20), and slowly advancing the needle 1 cun. Then perform lifting with force for 3 times (each lifting should take out the needle for no more than 0. 1 cun). This manipulation can be performed repeatedly. When Dingnie Qianxiexian is needled, same manipulation can be applied. During manipulating the needle, both hands can be used to lift the needles on two sides simultaneously. Retain the needles for 2 to 24 hours, during which the needles can be manipulated 3 to 5 times.

Or the method of vibration needling can be performed: When the needling sensation is obtained, retain the needle for 1 minute, then retreat 1/3 of the needle and perform slight lifting, twirling and thrusting with vibrating the needle meanwhile for 9 times (altogether 81 times) before the needle is withdrawn.

c. Therapeutic course

One treatment is given everyday or every other day. 10

treatments make one therapeutic course. An interval of 5 to 7 days between two courses is necessary.

d. Exercises

During manipulating the needle on Dingzhongxian, the patient is asked to perform certain conscious imaginations, such as recovery of the disease ... When Upper 1/5 of Dingnie Qianxiexian is needled, think about the movement of the toes — first the big toe, then the others. To support the conscious activity, some passive movement can also be conducted, such as raising the leg. Similar activities can be performed for the upper arms when Middle 2/5 of the Dingnie Qianxiexian is needled. During the conscious activities, the patient should concentrate his mind and get rid of all the distracting thoughts.

3) Skin needling

a. Point selection

(a) Huatuojiaji points from V_{4-6} of the injured part, Shenshu (BL 23), Baliao (Eight-Liao), Yinmen (BL 37), Weizhong (BL 40), Kunlun (BL 60)

(b) Qihai (RN 6), Tianshu (ST 25), Biguan (ST 31), Fengshi (GB 31), Zusanli (ST 36), Jiexi (ST 41)

(c) Huantiao (GB 30), Fengshi (GB 31), Yanglingquan (GB 34), Xuanzhong (GB 39), Qiuxu (GB 40).

For urinary incontinence, points on the medial part of both legs are added.

b. Manipulation

These 3 groups of points can be used alternately. Tapping with plum-blossom needle should be performed with light or moderate stimulation until local redness appears.

c. Therapeutic course

Same as above.

4) Electrotherapy

Prescription 1

a. Point selection

1 to 2 points of Du Meridian on the spinous process above

and below the cross section and the corresponding Huatuojiaji points can be taken as main points, which are supported by Biguan (ST 31), Futu (LI 18), Zusanli (ST 36), Jiexi (ST 41), Yanglingquan (GB 34), Shenshu (BL 23), Ciliao (BL 32), Weizhong (BL 40), Chengshan (BL 57).

For those with disturbance in urination and defecation Zhibian (BL 54), and Zhongji (RN 3) should be added.

b. Manipulation

These points are needled about 1 to 1.5 cun in depth. After deqi, withdraw the needles a little bit and connect the needle in Du points and Huatoujiaji points on the same side to the two poles of a G-6805 electric stimulator using low frequency and the continuous wave for 15—20 minutes. When the main points are needled, the patient lies in prone position, and when the adjunct points are needled in supine position, usually 2 to 4 main points can be used alternately. When Zhibian is needled, the inserting direction should be slightly deviate to the medial side.

c. Therapeutic course

The treatment is given once every other day. 15 treatments make one therapeutic course. An interval of 5 to 7 days should be arranged between two courses.

Prescription 2

a. Point selection

Yaoyangguan (DU 3), Shiqizhui (EX-B 8), Yaoshu (DU 2), and corresponding Huatoujiaji points, supported by Ciliao (BL 32), Huantiao (GB 30), Zhibian (BL 54), Chengfu (BL 36), Yinmen (BL 37), Jianxi, Zusanli (ST 36), Yanglingquan (GB 34), Juegu (GB 39).

For those with urinary incontinence, Guanyuan (RN 4), Zhongji (RN 3) and Sanyinjiao (SP 6) are added.

b. Manipulation

In each treatment, 4 to 5 points mainly from the Du Meridian and the Huatoujiaji points should be selected. The treatment can be given with the above-mentioned method once everyday.

c. Therapeutic course

Same as above.

Prescription 3

a. Point selection

For paralysis of the upper limbs: from Waiguan (SJ 5) to Neiguan (PC 6), Quchi (LI 11), Waibizhong [1 cun above Sidu (SJ 9)]

For paraplegia: from Sanyinjiao (SP 6) to Jugu (GB 39), Zusanli (ST 36), Siqiang (4.5 cun above the midpoint of upper margin of patella)

b. Manipulation

A filiform needle of 1.5 to 2 cun long is used. After deqi by lifting, thrusting, twirling and rotating, connect the needle to the electric stimulator discharging continuous wave and the stimulation should be tolerable to the patient. During treatment usually a rhythmic jerking on the affected limbs can be noticed. Retain the needle for 30 to 60 minutes. After the needle is withdrawn, suspended moxibustion should be applied over Zusanli for 1 to 2 minutes.

c. Therapeutic course

One treatment is given everyday. 7 treatments constitute one therapeutic course.

5) Point injection

Prescription 1

a. Point selection

Yaoshu (DU 2), Baliao, Zhibian (BL 54), Yinmen (BL 37), Futu (LI 18), Zusanli (ST 36), Yanglingquan (GB 34); Guanyuan (RN 4), Zhongji (RN 3)

b. Manipulation

In treating paraplegia, injections of Vitamin B group, Danggui (Chinese Angelica Root), Adenosine Triphosphate (ATP) and Strychnine Nitrate can be used. For urinary incontinence, Carbamylcholini Chloridum, Scopolamine Hydrobromide is used.

In selecting points, points of the Du Meridian, Bladder Meridian, and Yangming Meridian are often taken to treat paralysis of the limbs, and points of the abdomen are taken to regulate urination and defecation. In each treatment, 1 to 3 points are selected. During the treatment, lifting and thrusting should be performed after the needle is inserted to a certain depth. After the arrival of qi (a sensation of soreness numbness, heaviness and distension), the drug can be injected. When Yaoshu and other Du points are needled, the insertion should not be too deep. When the Shu points on the abdomen are needled, the bladder should be emptied first. The withdrawal of needle should be made swiftly. The points should be used alternately. The dosage for each point is about 0.5 to 1 ml.

   c. Therapeutic course

   The treatment is given once everyday or once every other day.

   Prescription 2

   a. Point selection

   Xuehai (SP 10), Zusanli (ST 36), Chengshan (BL 57), Shenshu (BL 23), Sanyinjiao (SP 6)

   b. Manipulation

   Same as mentioned above. The dosage for each point is 0.5—6 ml. The points can be used alternatively.

   c. Therapeutic course

   Same as above.

   6) Laser irradiation

   a. Point selection

   Mingmen (DU 4), Yaoyangguan (DU 3), Ciliao (BL 32), Yinlingquan (SP 9), Sanyinjiao (SP 6), Qihai (RN 6), Guanyuan (RN 4), Zhongji (RN 3)

   b. Manipulation

   A He-Ne laser therapy apparatus with a power of 10 mw and a light spot diameter of 2 mm is adopted. Each point is irradiated for 4 to 8 minutes in each treatment.

c. Therapeutic course

The treatment is given once every other day. 10 treatments make one therapeutic course. A spacing of one week between two courses should be arranged.

3. Therapeutic Effect

1) With the methods of " 9 points-needling on the cross section" in association with point injection, Dr. Li Guanrong treated 71 cases of spastic paraplegia, 53 cases of flaccid paraplegia and 124 cases of traumatic paraplegia. The duration of disease ranged from 2 months to 15 years. And all are complicated with disturbance of urination and defection. The over-all therapeutic results are satisfactory: 10 cases were cured (8.06%), 102 cases effective (82.26%), and 12 cases (9.68%) ineffective. The total effective rate was 90.32%. It is generally considered that the therapeutic results for flaccid paraplegia is rather better. (Journal of TCM, 1985; 12:26)

2) Paraplegia is generally caused by insufficient kidney-qi, and the pathogenic wind invading the weakened Du Meridian. The superficiality lies in Foot-Yangming, and the origin is in Foot-Shaoyin. The treatment should aim to needle Back Shu point first, then the points of the abdomen and the feet, so as to reinforce the kidney and the spinal cord, and to warm the tendon and dredge the collaterals. With this method, the therapeutic effect can be increased greatly, Dr. Chen Weicang treated 8 cases of paraplegia caused by myelitis with this method. After an average treatment of 30 times, 5 cases were cured and 3 cases improved. (Journal of TCM, 1981; 11:22)

3) The author had treated a case of high paraplegia with scalp acupuncture supported by filiform needling and electrotherapy with good result. Dr. Zhu Mingqing once treated a case of flaccid paraplegia on both lower limbs after surgery for tumor of spinal cord with scalp acupuncture. Only after one therapeutic course, the patient could walk around without the aid of crutches. (Dr. Zhu's Scalp Needling, Dongyang Pub. House, Japan.

1989; p. 181—182)

Dr. Li Guanrong et al. studied the EEG changes of the patients with paraplegia. They found that the scalp acupuncture has a very good effect on the regulation of the metabolism of the nerve cells. It can make the brain change from a state of excitement to a state of inhibition. Therefore, its effect of nourishing yin and suppressing the sthenic yang is apparent. The scalp acupuncture with certain kind of manipulating methods can play an important role in influencing the central nervous system. The meridians and collaterals can be dredged and qi-blood circulation can be adjusted by the needling.

4) Dr. Han Yuju treated 374 cases of paraplegia with point irradiation combined with other therapeutic measures. The results showed that 9.9% of the cases were basically cured; 21.7% obtained very satisfactory effect; 56.1% were improved and 12.3% were with no effect. It has been considered that Vitamins of B group, ATP and Strychnine have a very good effect on the nourishment and excitement of the nervous system, and Scopolamine can play an important role in improving and relaxing the spasm of the detrusor muscle of bladder. (Journal of Chinese Acupuncture, 1987; 6:7)

According to Dr. Li Guanrong, the injection of Safflower and Chinese Angelica Root have a very good effect on promoting blood circulation and removing blood stasis, clearing and activating the meridians and collaterals. It can also improve the local blood flow, and accelerate the recovery of the functions of the peripheral nerve. (Journal of TCM, 1985; 12:26)

5) Through the action of He-Ne laser's light guide fibre on the Jingluo points, laser irradiation can carry out the comprehensive therapeutic effect of laser, needling and moxibustion. It can help dilate the blood vessels, promote metabolism and improve the general or local symptoms of the patient with paraplegia. This therapeutic method can be used together with other acupuncture methods.

4. Discussion

1) Acupuncture treatment is effective for paraplegia caused by spinal injury, tuberculosis of spine and acute myelitis, but has no effect on the paraplegia caused by the compression of tumors.

2) Better therapeutic effect can be obtained if acupuncture is given at the convalescent stage after the primary disease is treated.

3) Though acupuncture has rather good therapeutic effect on paraplegia, it in most cases, is used together with other therapeutic measures such as laser irradiation, electric therapy ... It's worth mentioning that no matter what kind of method is adopted, functional exercises must be stressed, which is very important to raise the effect.

4) Dr. Gao Xipeng revealed that there was possibility for human spinal cord to regenerate after injury, and the nerve function can be restored. Modern medicine tells us that most of the spinal injury in peace time do not belong to the type of dismember anatomically. But severe injury to the spinal cord may cause the disappearance of motor and sensory functions below the injury. It is generally considered that there are very few chances for the paraplegia that lasts over 24 hours to be recovered automatically. However, he had cured four patients who had suffered from traumatic complete paraplegia with acupuncture therapy. The function of their nervous system had been restored gradually. This shows that the severed transmission route is reconnected. He thinks that a correct diagnosis and a proper treatment are the necessary for the regeneration of the spinal cord. Meanwhile, the potentiality of spinal regeneration depends, at least partly, on the age of the patient, i.e. the immature nervous system has better opportunity to regenerate. (Chinese Acupuncture, 1985; 5:5)

5) Satisfactory therapeutic effect can also be achieved in those paralysed patients who have missed the timely operations

and those who had become completely paralysed long after the operation. In this case of course, the treatment may require several therapeutic courses or last even several years. The patient should be patient and very cooperate with the doctors.

SECTION III
Quadriplegia

Quadriplegia refers to paralysis of both the upper and lower limbs. Besides the high paraplegia caused by diseases of the cervical spinal cord, there is also the paraplegia caused by diseases of the lower motor neuron, which is commonly seen in polyneuritis. The disease may be also seen in myasthenia gravis. In most cases, there is a morbid fatigue history of the eyes, face and throat, and progressive myodystrophy (atrophy and weakness of the proximal muscles of the four limbs), multiple myositis (may be complicated by myalgia and skin diseases). Acute infective multiple radiculoneuritis is a special type of multiple neuritis which may lead to symmetrical flaccid paralysis of the four limbs.

Though the method of "treating different disease with the same therapeutic principle" can be used in treating quadriplegia, "Bianzheng Lunzhi (Treating the disease based on differentiation)" is of the utmost importance.

1. Polyneuritis

Also known as peripheral neuritis or multiple neuritis and it refers to the symmetrical involvements of motor, sensory and autonomic nerves in the distal regions of the four limbs. It is a kind of flaccid paralysis and dystrophy, and is mainly caused by general infection, malnutrition, metabolic disturbance of such factors as metals and drugs. Desmosis and cancers are sometimes causes of this disease.

Polyneuritis belongs to "arthralgia-syndrome" or "flaccidity-syndrome" in TCM.

Clinical Manifestation

1) Acute, subacute or chronic onset.

2) Distension and numbness or pain and formication in the hands and feet which gradually spread to the trunk.

3) Symmetrical typical sensory disturbance like glove/sock-anesthesia or burning pain in distal limbs.

4) Symmetrical hypomyodynamia, hypomyotonia, decrease or disappearance of tendon reflex, and myodynia in the distal parts of the limbs, After the acute stage, there will be muscular atrophy.

5) There is also cold sensation in the distal end of the limbs where the skin becomes smooth, thin, dry, rugous or chapped. Nails become loose with hyperkeratosis, and the limbs may perspire more than usual.

6) The disease is characterized by symmetrical distribution in both limbs. The symptoms in the distal end are more obvious than that in the proximal part.

7) The disease caused by arsenic poisoning may lead to more serious damage to the lower limbs, such as severe pain and decreased or disappeared deep sensory sensation. That caused by lead poisoning may have wrist drop due to the injury of the radial nerve. In beriberi there is both disturbance in sensory and motor functions. Generally the symptoms of the lower limbs are more serious than that of the upper limbs. There is apparent tenderness of gastrocnemius muscle.

Acupuncture Treatment

1) Filiform needle needling

a. Point selection

The upper limbs: Jianyu (LI 15), Quchi (LI 11), Waiguan (SJ 5), Hegu (LI 4), Baxie (EX-UE 9)

The lower limbs: Huantiao (GB 30), Zusanli (ST 36), Xuanzhong (GB 39), Sanyinjiao (SP 6), Bafeng (EX-LE 10)

b. Manipulation

Make deep insertion and induce moderate stimulation with a No. 26 or 28 filiform needle of 2 cun long. Or use needle of a diameter of 0. 8 to 1. 0 mm (about 3—8 cun long) and the hand (foot) needle of a diameter of 0. 4 to 0. 5 mm (2—3 cun long) can be used to needle the points on the limbs or hands (feet) respectively. During the needling, make the insertion shallow first, then deep with slow pressing. Twirling and rotating should combine with lifting and thrusting until there is an electric shock sensation. Retain the needle for 10 minutes. There is no need to press the needle hole after withdrawal if there is no bleeding.

c. Therapeutic course

The treatment is given once a day or once every other day. 15 to 30 treatments make one therapeutic course.

2) Ear acupuncture

a. Point selection

Points corresponding to the disease site, sympathetic part, Shenmen

b. Manipulation

After sterilized, the selected points may be stimulated lightly with a filiform needle. Retain the needle for 10—15 minutes during which the needle can be manipulated several times.

c. Therapeutic course

The treatment is given once everyday or once every other day. 10 treatments constitute one therapeutic course. A spacing of 5 to 7 mays may be arranged between two courses.

3) Scalp acupuncture

a. point selection

Upper 1/5 and Middle 2/5 of the Dingnie Qianxiexian; Upper 1/5 and Middle 2/5 of the Dingnie Houxiexian

b. Manipulation

Insert 3 needles one by one on the Dingnie Qianxiexian to the cross-point of Middle 2/5 and Lower 2/5. Then needle Dingnie Houxiexian with the following two methods: (a) Make relay insertions with 3 needles on Dingnie Houxiexian. (b) Penetrate 3 needles from Dingnie Qianxiexian to Dingnie Houxiexian. The method of "qi withdrawal" should be adopted in both needling methods.

c. Therapeutic course

The treatment is given once every other day. 10 treatments constitute one therapeutic course. A spacing of 5 to 7 days should be arranged between two courses.

4) Skin needling

a. Point selection

Huatoujiaji points mainly T_{1-4}, positive areas of the lumbosacral part and the affected regions of the limbs. Adjunct points: the medial and lateral sides of the forearm, the palm, the dorsum of hand and finger tips for disease of the upper arm; and the medial and lateral sides of the leg, the dorsum of foot and toe tips for disease of the lower limb.

b. Manipulation

Tap the points and the affected parts with moderate or heavy stimulation until the local skin becomes reddish with no bleeding or with a little bleeding. But there is some bleeding when the tips of fingers and toes are needled with pricking method.

c. Therapeutic course

The treatment is given once everyday or once every other day. 10 to 15 treatments constitute one therapeutic course. An interval of 2 to 3 weeks is required between two courses.

5) Point injection

a. Point selection

Same as the points selected for filiform needle needling.

b. Manipulation

In each treatment, 2 to 4 points are selected and 0.5 to 1 ml of Vit. B_1, B_2 or B_{12} is injected into each point.

c. Therapeutic course

One treatment is given every other day. A therapeutic course consists of 10 treatments.

Therapeutic Effect

1) The author had treated this disease with filiform needle needling. After deqî, connect the needles with a G-6805 stimulator for 15 minutes. The therapeutic results are satisfactory, especially for the patient in the early period of disease and those disease with shorter duration. The patients can be cured without any sequelae. However to those longstanding cases, the therapeutic effect is not so ideal, or even not effective at all.

2) Dr. Guan Haiqi treated 36 cases with thick needles. The curative rate was 63.89%; remarkable improvement rate 22.22%, and improvement rate 11.11. The over-all effective rate was 97.22%. (Chinese Acupuncture, 1982; 6:14)

Discussion

1) The disease should be treated according to the etiology and symptom differentiation. Nutrition of the patient should be improved properly.

2) Patience is necessary because the recovery from disease is rather slow. Generally a combined form of acupuncture therapy would achieve better results.

3) For patients difficult in walking or other movement, besides needling, physiotherapy, physical exercise therapy, drug administration should be given as a supplementary measure to raise the therapeutic results.

2. Acute Infective Multiple Radiculoneuritis

Acute infective multiple radiculoneuritis, also known as Green-Bali Syndrome, is a special kind of multiple neuritis, which can be found in any age group and in any season. It may be caused by virus infection, and the allergic reaction to virus/germ infection and prophylactic vaccination or caused by autoimmune reaction. The disease mainly invades the peripheral nerves, the nerve root, and in a few cases, the anterior horn of spinal cord and the motor nuclei of the brain stem.

Clinical Manifestation

1) There is history of infections of the upper respiratory tract or diarrhea before the onset of disease.

2) The initial symptoms include symmetrical weakness of the limbs either starting from the distal or proximal end, and finally involving the whole limb. Both the distal and the proximal ends may also be involved simultaneously. Sometimes, the trunk is also involved. Respiratory paralysis can be found in some serious cases because of the involvement of the intercostal muscles and the diaphragmatic muscle.

3) the paralysis is flaccid in nature. The tendon reflex decreases or disappears but there is no pathological reflex. There exists apparent tenderness in the affected muscles.

4) At the early stage of the disease, the muscular atrophy is not very apparent. Those with serious symptoms may have muscular atrophy, especially in the distal regions of the affected limbs.

5) The sensory disturbance is milder than the motor disturbance. It often show itself as glove/sock anesthesia in the distal region of the limbs. Some patients may complaint severe pain. However, some cases may show no sensory disturbance.

6) The cranial nerves, most commonly bilateral facial nerves are involved. In addition, there will be paralysis of the glossopharyngeal nerve and the vagus nerve with such symptoms of bulbar paralysis as dyslalia, dysphagia ... The disease may also be accompanied by paralysis of the eye muscles.

7) There will be heart failure if the cardiac muscle is involved.

8) Cerebrospinal fluid examination show separation between the cells and the proteins, namely, the number of cells is normal or slightly increased, while the protein increases from 50—100 mg% to over 200 mg%, or even 1000 mg%. The increase of protein often appears 7—10 days after the onset and reaches its peak at third week, and gradually gets down to normal after 6

weeks. Some patients may show normal cerebrospinal fluid in the whole course of disease.

9) In about two thirds of the cases, the transmission speed of the motor nerves in the distal end of the limbs is about 60% lower than normal. The amplitude of the muscular action potential seen in electromyography may be normal, but that of the proximal end may become lowered. In about one third of the cases, the transmission speed of the motor nerve in the distal end is normal, but is lowered in the proximal end.

Therapeutic Methods

When the disease conditions become stable, acupuncture treatment can be applied. The points are mainly selected from the Hand/Foot Yangming Meridian.

1) Filiform needle needling

a. Point selection

In the upper limb: Shousanli (LI 10), Hegu (LI 4). The adjunct points are Jianyu (LI 15), Jianliao (SJ 14), Jianzhen (SI 9), Quchi (LI 11), Waiguan (SJ 5)

In the lower limb: Shenshu (BL 23), Dachangshu (BL 25), Huantiao (GB 30). The adjunct points are Zhibian (BL 54), Biguan (ST 31), Zusanli (ST 36), Yanglingquan (GB 34), Xuanzhong (GB 39), Kunlun (BL 60)

In the trunk: Huatoujiaji points, Ganshu (BL 18), Pishu (BL 20), Shenshu (BL 23)

For dysphagia: Lianquan (RN 23), Yamen (DU 15), Renying (ST 9)

For facial paralysis: Dicang (ST 4), Jiache (ST 6), Yifeng (SJ 17), Sibai (ST 2)

b. Manipulation

For babies, swift insertion should be practiced without retaining needle. Usually reinforcing method is applied.

For children patients, the needle can be retained for 15 to 20 minutes.

c. Therapeutic course

One treatment is given everyday. 10 to 15 treatments constitute one therapeutic course. A spacing of 2 to 3 days should be arranged between two courses.

2) Needle warming with moxibustion

a. Point selection

Same as Filiform needle needling.

b. Manipulation

After deqi, reinforcing method is practiced by lifting, thrusting, twirling and rotating. Cast a moxa stick on the needle body until it is about 2—3 cm apart from the skin. Burn the moxa stick from the lower end. The needle can be withdrawn a little while after the stick is burned out.

c. Therapeutic course

One treatment is given every other day. 10 to 15 treatments constitute one therapeutic course. A spacing of 2 to 3 days should be arranged between two courses.

3) Needling with thick needle

a. Point selection

From Dazhui (DU 14) to Shenzhu (BL 23); from Shendao (DU 11) to Zhiyang (DU 9).

For paralysis of the upper limbs: Zhongfu (LU 1), Shousanli (LI 10), Neiguan (PC 6) and Hegu (LI 4) are added.

For paralysis of the lower limbs: Huantiao (GB 30), Yinmen (BL 37) and Chengshan (BL 57) are added.

b. Manipulation

Penetration needling is applied to the main points with a thick needle (diameter: 0.8 mm). Retain the needle for 2 hours. The adjunct points are also needled with thick needle (diameter: 0.4 mm). No retaining of needle is needed. Apply heavy stimulation.

c. Therapeutic course

Same as above.

4) Scalp acupuncture

a. Point selection

For paralysis of the upper limb, add Middle 2/5 of Dingnie

Qianxiexian.

For paralysis of the lower limb, add Upper 1/5 Dingnie Qianxiexian.

For facial paralysis, add Lower 2/5 of Dingnie Qianxiexian and Nieqianxian.

For sensory disturbance of the upper limb: Middle 2/5 of Dingnie Houxiexian is added.

For sensory disturbance of the lower limb: Upper 1/5 of Dingnie Houxian is added.

b. Manipulation

Reducing by "qi withdrawal" should be performed when a No. 30 filiform needle of 1.5 cun long is inserted into the lower layer of the aponeurosis. Retain the needle for 2 to 24 hours.

c. Therapeutic course.

The treatments can be given once everyday or once every other day. 10 treatments make one therapeutic course. The interval between two courses is 5 to 7 days.

d. Exercises

During needling, the conscious movement should be combined with the active or passive limb movement. For example, when Dingzhongxian or the Upper 1/5 Dingnie Qianxiexian are needled, the patient should concentrate his minds on the affected area of the lower limb. No matter whether the patient can or can not move his diseased limb, he should imagine that the disease had already been cured, that is, to support the treatment consciously. Those who can move the limb should practice various kind of exercises such as raising the leg, extending the knee and bending the toes. If he can not move his diseased limb, passive exercises should also be practiced under the help of others. During the needle is retained, similar activities must also be conducted.

5) Point injection

a. Point selection

Same as Filiform needle needling.

b. Manipulation

4 to 6 points can be taken. After deqi, inject in each point 0.5 ml of a mixture of Adenosine Triphosphate, Coenzyme A, Vit. B_1, Vit. B_2, Galanthamine and Novocain (each with an amount of a standard ampule).

c. Therapeutic course

The treatment is given once every other day. 15 treatments constitute one therapeutic course. The spacing between two courses is 2 to 3 days.

Needling and Point injection can be applied in turn.

Therapeutic Effect

1) Based on the paralysed muscles, the points can be selected mainly from the Hand- or Foot-Yangming Meridian. Those from the Hand- or Foot-Shaoyang and Foot-Taiyang Meridians can be taken as adjunct points. Usually satisfactory therapeutic effect can be obtained. Dr. Zhao Lan treated 50 cases with the acupuncture associated with point injection. As a result, 23 cases cured, 16 cases apparently improved and 11 cases improved. The over-all effective rate was 100%. (Chinese Acupuncture, 1983; 3:7)

2) At the same time when needling therapy is performed, massage and functional exercises should be conducted to raise the therapeutic effect.

Discussion

1) In the needling treatment, points can be needled in an order from proximal to distal part. Take the upper limb as an example, points in the shoulder, then the upper arm, elbow, forearm and the hand are needled successively.

2) Dr. Shi Bingde claimed that the disease should be treated with combined ways. Examples are as follows:

For paralysis of upper limb with difficulty in raising the arms: Dazhui, Jianjing, Jianzhong, Jianyu, Jianliao, Binao and Jubi (3.5 cun inferior and anterior to acromion) are taken.

For weakness in extending the elbow: Gongzhong, Jianzhen

and Quchi are taken.

For weakness in flexing the elbow: Quchi, Chize, Quze, Bizhong (the midpoint on the line between carpal skin striation and the cubital skin striation) are selected.

For those with wrist drop: Quchi, Shousanli, Sixu, Waiguan are needled.

For difficulty in extending and flexing the fingers: Jianshi, Neiguan, Shenmen, Hegu, Waiguan and Baxie are selected.

For paralysed lower limb with difficulty in raising the leg: Dachangshu, Shenshu, Huantiao, Chongmen, Biguan and Futu can be selected.

For flexion contracture of the hip joints and knee joints: Shenji (0.5 cun aside of the lower aspect of the second lumbar spinous process): Yinmen, Xiyangguan, Fengshi and Heding are needled.

For weakness in thigh abduction: Huatuojiaji L_4 and L_5, Juliao, and Tiaoyao (2 cun below the highest point of iliac crest) are taken.

For weakness in hip adduction: Jimai, Yinlian, Xuehai, and Qimen are taken.

For weakness in flexing the knee: Chengfu, Yinmen, Weizhong and Huantiao are needled.

For weakness in extending the knee: Chongmen, Biguan, Futu, Siqiang (4.5 cun above the midpoint of the upper margin of the patella) are taken.

For foot drop: Zusanli, Shangjuxu, Xiajuxu, Jiexi, Taichong and Xiachuidian (3 cun above Jiexi , 1 cun lateral to the external border of tibia) are needled.

For foot eversion: Yinlian, Sanyinjiao, Taixi and Jiuwaifan (1 cun aside of the medial side of Chengshan) are taken.

For foot inversion: Yanglingquan, Xuanzhong, Xiajuxi, Qiuxu, and Jiuneifan (1 cun aside of the external side of Chengshan) are needled.

For talipes calcaneus: Weizhong, Chengshan, Genping (the cross point of the line of medial-lateral malleolus and the

Achilles tendon: Kunlun and Taixi are needled.

For difficulty in flexion and extension of toes: Jiexi, Tai-chong, Bafeng, Weizhong and Chengshan are selected.

When hydro-acupuncture therapy is adopted, usually the mixture of Vit. B_1, B_{12}, Chinese Angelica Root Compound or Red Sage Root Compound, Coenzyme A, ATP, and Galan-thamine are used for injections. In each treatment, 2 to 4 kind of the above drugs are selected and 4 to 8 points are selected. 0. 5 ml. of the mixture is injected into each point. The treatment is given once every other day. 10 treatments constitute one thera-peutic course. The spacing between two courses is 7 to 10 days. Generally 4 to 8 courses are needed. The points for electrothera-py are selected based on the distribution of nerves in the injured muscles. In each electric treatment, 2 to 4 pairs of points are needled for 10 to 15 minutes with continuous waves. The stimu-lation should be enough to induce the muscular contraction. The treatment is given once every other day. 10 treatments constitute one therapeutic course. The interval between two courses is 7 to 10 days. When catgut embedding therapy is applied, 3 to 4 points are selected in each treatment and No. 1 catgut is often used. The treatment is given once everyday until the disorder is cured. In treating patients with light paralysis (myodynamics: over grade III), the point injection and electric needling can beadopted alternately if any of them is used independently with unsatisfactory effect after a treatment of 2 to 3 therapeutic cours-es. For those with serious paralysis (myodynamics: below grade II) or those with a disease course of over 6 months, point catgut ligation therapy and point catgut embedding therapy can be adopted if no satisfactory therapies for 3 to 6 therapeutic cours-es. According to a clinical observation on 617 cases of infantile flaccidity syndrome, among whom there were 49 cases belonging to acute multiple radiculoneuritis, it was found that the thera-peutic effect in this kind of paralysis is better than the paralysis caused by injury of the cerebrospinal nerves and poliomyelitis.

3) Nursing should be strengthened to prevent from bed

sore, pulmonary infection and limb deformity.

3. Myasthenia Gravis

Myasthenia gravis is a chronic disease due to disturbance of the conductive functions in the neuromuscular junction. The disease may first attack the muscle in the eyes, face and throat, then the muscles in the four limbs.

Clinical Manifestation

In most cases, the disease starts at the age between 20 to 30 years and is more common in females. According to the area involved, the disease can be divided into three types. But some may be a mixed type.

1) Eye muscle type

This type of myasthenia gravis is more common in children, whose main symptoms include squint, double vision or immovable eyeballs caused by blepharoptosis and paralysis of musculus rectus lateralis oculi. In a long-standing disease, the disease may gradually involve the muscles modulated by medulla oblongata and the skeletal muscles of the whole body.

2) Medulla oblongata muscle type

The symptoms are dyslalia, choking, progressive lowering voice, masticatory atonia, dysphagia, facial apathy ... etc. In severe cases, there is dyspnea which may endanger the life.

3) Systemic type

More common in male patients after middle age. With an acute onset, clinical symptoms are extreme muscular fatigue and difficulty in swallowing, breathing and turning the body. It will endanger the life of the patient if emergent treatment is not given actively.

4) The muscular asthenia is mild in the morning, but becomes more serious in the afternoon or evening (especially more serious after physical labor, but can be relieved after a rest). The examination on nervous system may find nothing abnormal.

5) The fatigue test for the involved muscles may show in-

creased muscular asthenia when quick and repeated movements are conducted. After a rest, this symptom can be improved or disappeared. The fatigue test for the long-standing cases are valueless because their symptoms may have already become fixed.

6) The anti-cholinesterase drug test: The diagnosis can be determined if the symptoms are improved dramatically half an hour to one hour after 0.5 to 1.5 ml of Neostigmine is injected into the affected muscle of a suspected case. (Sometimes 0.6 ml of Atropine Sulfate is added.) If there is such muscarinic reactions as pallor , sweating , salivation , abdominal pain . . . etc , Atropine can be used to relieve the symptoms.

7) Electric stimulation test: If there is no muscular contraction in a short period of time when the injured muscle is stimulated by constant electric current, it is called myasthenic reaction, and a correct diagnosis is established.

Acupuncture Treatment

1) Filiform needle needling

Prescription 1

a. Point selection

Zhongwan (RN 12), Qihai (RN 6), Sanyinjiao (SP 6), Zusanli (ST 36) and Xuehai (SP 10) are taken as the main points.

For paralysis of the levator muscle of the upper eyelid, add Zanzhu (BL 2), Yuyao (EX-HN 4), Tongziliao (GB 1), and Sizhukong (SJ 23). This can also be supported by needling the adjunct points such as Taiyang (KI 1), Hegu (LI 4) and Fengchi (GB 20).

For paralysis of the musculus rectus medialis oculi, such main points as Zanzhu (BL 2), Jingming (BL 1), Yuyao (EX-HN 4), Yangbai (GB 14), and such adjunct points as Hegu (LI 4), Chengqi (ST 1), Sibai (ST 2), are added.

For paralysis of the upper oblique muscle, the main points Zanzhu (BL 2), Jingming (BL 1), Qiuhou (EX-HN 7) and the adjunct points Hegu (LI 4), Yangbai (GB 14), Chengqi (ST 1),

Taiyang (KI 1) are added.

For paralysis of the whole eye muscles, Qiuhou (EX-HN 7), Jingming (BL 1), Zanzhu (BL 2), Sizhukong (SJ 23) and the adjunct points Chengqi (ST 1), Taiyang (KI 1), Yuyao (EX-HN 4), are added.

For dysphagia of the medulla oblongata muscle type, Fengchi (GB 20), Tiantu (RN 22), Lianquan (RN 23), Yamen (DU 15), are added.

For dyslalia and dysphonia, Yamen (DU 15) and Lianquan (RN 23) are added.

For the disease of systemic type, Jianyu (LI 15), Quchi (LI 11), Waiguan (SJ 5), Hegu (LI 4), Huantiao (GB 30), Fengshi (GB 31), Yanglingquan (GB 34) and Taichong (LR 3) are added.

b. Manipulation

In each treatment 2 to 3 main points and 2 to 3 adjunct points are grouped and needled alternately. The filiform needles of 1 to 1. 5 cun long are used to induce reinforcement by lifting, thrusting, twirling and rotating. The needles are retained for 15 to 30 minutes.

c. Therapeutic course

One treatment is given everyday. 6 treatments constitute one therapeutic course. The spacing between two courses is 2 days.

Prescription 2

a. Point selection

The main points: Baihui (DU 20), Danzhong (RN 17), Zusanli (ST 36)

The adjunct points: Yangbai (GB 14), Zanzhu (BL 2), Jingming (BL 1), Yuyao (EX-HN 4), Sizhukong (SJ 23), Sibai (ST 2)

b. Manipulation

All the points except Zusanli should be selected from the affected side and needled by shallow needling with a filiform needle of 0.5 to 1 cun long. Zusanli should be needled perpendicularly on both sides with a filiform needle of 1.5 cun long. The needle should be retained for 20 minutes.

c. Therapeutic course

Same as above.

2) Scalp acupuncture

a. Point selection

Dingzhongxian, Upper 1/5 Dingnie Qianxiexian, and Middle 2/5 of Zhengshang Pangxian

b. Manipulation

Reinforcing by qi entering is used on Dingzhongxian and reducing by "qi withdrawal" is applied on Dingnie Qianxiexian and Zhengshang Pangxian. Retain the needle for 2 to 24 hours during which the needles are manipulated 1 or 2 times. After deqi, the needle can also be connected with a g-6805 stimulator for 15 minutes. The frequency used is between 50 to 100/minute.

c. Therapeutic course

One treatment everyday or every other day. 10 treatments make one therapeutic course. The spacing between two courses is 3 to 5 days.

3) Ear needling

a. Point selection

The main points: Subcortex, Spleen, Eye

The adjunct points: Liver, Endocrine, Kidney

b. Manipulation

In each treatment, 3 to 4 points on both ears are needled with a filiform needle of 0.5 cun long. Manipulate the needle every five minutes by twirling the needle leftward and rightward. The needles are retained for 30 minutes.

c. Therapeutic course.

Same as above.

4) Point injection

a. Point selection

Quchi (LI 11), Waiguan (SJ 5), Hegu (LI 4), Fengshi (GB 31), Xuehai (SP 10), Zusanli (ST 36), Yinlingquan (SP

9), Yanglingquan (GB 34), Sanyinjiao (SP 6)

    b. Manipulation

In each treatment, 2 to 3 points (both sides) are selected. After deqi, inject one ml of the mixture of Vit. B_1 and B_{12} to each point.

    c. Therapeutic course

Same as above.

Therapeutic Effect

It has been found that acupuncture is effective to myasthenia gravis. Dr. Ju Guiqin treated the disease by filiform needle needling with a curative rate of 95.3%, an improvement rate of 1.6% and no effect rate of 3.1%. (Journal of Shanghai Acupuncture, 1980; 3:7)

Dr. Huo Jinshan treated 3 cases of myasthenia gravis by shallow needling plus massage on Baihui (DU 20), Danzhong (RN 17), Fengchi (GB 20), Ganshu (BL 18) and Pishu (BL 20) in an attempt to regulate the Zang-fu, balance yin and yang and raise the immunological functions of the body. As a result. all the 3 cases were cured. (Journal of TCM, 1990; 5:31)

Dr. Ye Zengui treated 16 cases of paralysis of the eye muscles with scalp acupuncture and electrotherapy. In the needling, some points around the eyes are selected. The result showed that 8 cases were cured and 7 cases were improved. (Journal of Chinese Acupuncture, 1984; 3:12)

Dr. Xu Rezhong reported his therapeutic results in Study on Ear Needling that this therapeutic method is effective to mild paralysis cases but no effect to systemic paralysis.

Discussion

1) According to TCM theory, the disease of myasthenia gravis can be divided into 3 types —— yin deficiency of the liver and kidney, qi deficiency of the spleen and stomach and deficiency of both qi and blood. In the needling treatment, the points can be selected according to the differentiation and the reinforc-

ing method should be adopted mainly.

2) Though acupuncture is effective for this disease, a long term treatment of more than half a year is necessary for the recovery. The therapeutic effect on the paralysis of the eye muscle type or of the trunk type is better than that of the systemic type or the medulla oblongata type. Acupuncture can be combined with herbal treatment to achieve better therapeutic effect.

3) A proper rest is important during the acupuncture treatment. Emotional excitement or various kind of infections should be avoided.

4) Those critical cases with systemic symptoms and signs such as myasthenia should be hospitalized and receive emergency treatment with Western medicinal measures. Any delay of the treatment will cause disaster.

4. Periodic Paralysis

Periodic paralysis is a kind of flaccid paralysis caused by disturbance of potassium metabolism, or in a few cases, by hereditary factors. It is characterized by repeated attacks, during which the potassium content in the muscle cells increased but decreased in serum. In some cases, the potassium concentration in the serum is also increased or remains unchanged. This disease may also be complicated by hyperthyroidism.

Clinical Manifestation

1) Hypokalemic periodic paralysis (very common)

a. The disease often occurs in male patients of 10 to 30 years old.

b. It often attacks the patient early in the morning or in the midnight when the patient wakes up. In most cases, the predisposing factors are overeating or strenuous exercise.

c. It is a kind of symmetric paralysis. The symptoms in the lower limbs are much more serious than the upper limbs. In severe cases, the muscles of the neck and trunk, the respiratory muscle or even the deglutition muscle would be involved.

d. There is attenuation or disappearance of the tendon reflex of the paralysed limbs.

e. The cardiac muscles may be involved with arrhythmia and decreased blood pressure.

f. After several hours or even several days, the paralysis can be improved gradually.

g. During the attack, the serum potassium is lower than 3 mEq/liter. The ECG also shows hypokalemia.

2) Hyperkalemia periodic paralysis (very rare)

a. Children often begin to have the disease at around 10.

b. The attack may be induced by strenuous exercise, coldness or sylvite drugs.

c. The symptoms are similar to those of hypokalemic paralysis. The disease may last for only several minutes to several hours with myalgia and muscular spasm.

d. In a few cases, there is myotonia of the muscles of the face and the tongue.

e. During the attack, serum potassium is higher than 5 mEq/liter. The ECG also show hyperkalemia.

3) Periodic paralysis with normal potassium content (very rare)

a. The clinical pictures are similar to hypokalemia paralysis. The disease may last for several days to several weeks.

b. The serum potassium is normal. The sylvite drugs is not effective to this disease.

Acupuncture Treatment

1) Filiform needle needling

a. Point selection

For paralysis of the upper limb: Zhongfu (LU 1), Shousanli (LI 10), Hegu (LI 4)

For paralysis of the lower limb: Zhibian (BL 54), Heyang (BL 55), Yanglingquan (GB 34), Zusanli (ST 36)

b. Manipulation

Induce strong stimulation with a diameter of 0.5 mm thick

needle. No retaining of needle is required.

c. Therapeutic course

The treatment is given once everyday or every other day. 10 treatments constitute one therapeutic course.

2) Scalp acupuncture

a. Point selection

For paralysis of the lower limb: Dingzhongxian, Upper 1/5 of Dingnie Qianxiexian, Dingpangxian I

For paralysis of the upper limb: dingzhongxian, Middle 2/5 of Dingnie Qianxiexian, Dingpangxian II

b. Manipulation

After entering the galea aponeurotica by rapid insertion, the needle is leveled and then the reducing method by "qi withdrawal" is conducted. The needle is retained for 2 to 12 hours, during which the needle can be manipulated several times.

c. Therapeutic course

Same as above.

d. Exercises

During needling and retaining of needle, the conscious activities should be practiced with passive or active movement of the affected limb.

Therapeutic Effect

Acupuncture is very effective for this disorder. According to *Thick Needle Needling*, patients with this disease can usually stand up and walk only with one treatment. Patients who accept the scalp acupuncture can also be cured with only one treatment. (Please refer to the typical cases report in Chapter Five)

SECTION IV
Monoparesis

Monoparesis refers to the paralysis of a single upper or lower limb. When the upper motor neurons are involved, it is mostly caused by the lesion in the motor cortex. In a few cases, the disease is caused by lesion in spinal cord. When the lower motor neurons are involved, the causes of monoparesis include poliomyelitis, syringomyelia, progressive spinal myodystrophia and injuries of the brachial nerve plexus.

In the treatment of monoparesis by acupuncture, the therapeutic methods often vary according to the different predisposing factors and different clinical manifestations.

1. Poliomyelitis

Poliomyelitis is an acute infectious disease caused by the poliovirus. The route of infection is mainly through digestive tract, but some through respiratory tract. The virus arriving the intestine or pharynges invade the local lymph nodes, where they got into the blood circulation and finally reach the central nervous system. With a direct hit to the motor nerve cells of the anterior horn of spinal gray and white matter, and cause edema and interrupt the blood flow. As a result, there will be anoxia or even necrosis of the nerve cells on the affected part. Clinically, there will be symptoms of paraplegia.

This disease is prevalent in summer and autumn in children between 1 to 5 years old. Some patients manifest symptom of flaccid paralysis, therefore, it is also named infantile paralysis.

The acute stage of this disease belongs to the category of "heat symptom complex" and after paralysis occurs in the limbs, it belongs to "flaccidity syndrome" in TCM.

Clinical Manifestation

1) Ask the contact history of the patient and ask if he or she has taken the oral poliomyelitis vaccine.

In summer or autumn, if a child who has never taken any poliomyelitis vaccine in the epidemic area, is found to suffer from one of the following symptoms, i. e. fever, headache, nausea, vomiting, pain in the leg or neck and hyperesthesia, poliomyelitis should be suspected.

2) During the onset, there will be general symptoms or symptoms in the digestive and respiratory tract, such as fever, sore throat, cough, poor appetite, diarrhea, sweating, ... After 1 to 4 days, the symptoms may vanish, but followed by headache, drowsiness, pain and numbness of the limbs, hyperesthesia, lumbosacral pain and fever again.

3) Slight symptoms of meningeal irritation may appear before paralysis occurs, such as stiffness in muscles of the back, failure to sit steadily and preference to support the trunk with the arms at the back. In babies, there may be fullness of the anterior fontanelle.

4) Paralysis often occur on the 2nd to the 5th day of the fever or on the 2nd to the 5th day of the second fever. The disease is characterized by flaccid paralysis which is unevenly and unsymmetrically distributed in the four limbs. It can be seen in any major muscle groups, especially in the larger muscle groups of the lower limbs. Paralysis of the proximal muscles is more common than that of the distal muscles. Though the tendon reflex disappears, sensory sensations still exist.

5) Besides the four limbs, paralysis can also occur in the back muscle (weakness in sitting), the abdominal muscle (protuberance of abdominal wall with disappearance of reflex) and the respiratory muscle (dyspnea and hypoxia).

6) Several days after the fever, there would be no further progress of paralysis. Recovery in most cases might be expected within 6 months to 1 year, but few cases may have such sequelae as atrophy and deformity of the limbs.

7) The sequelae mainly include paraplegia (disturbance of the motor function), weakness (laxation of the ligament, hypomyotonia), pathogenic leanness (myophagism), coldness (lowered skin temperature), and deformity (contracture of tendon, deformity of joints, inability in movement).

8) Identification should be made between poliomyelitis and multiple radiculoneuritis. The latter has no such prodromal symptoms as fever, and the paralysis develop gradually for sev-

eral weeks to involve the whole limbs. It is often of a bilateral and symmetric nature with sensory disturbance.

9) Examination of the cerebrospinal fluid is normal, or shows increase of cells (no more than $500/mm^3$ and mainly lymphocytes). There is light increase of the proteins and nothing significant can be found in biochemical aspect.

10) Virus isolation from cerebrospinal fluid and feces can confirm the diagnosis.

Acupuncture Treatment

Acupuncture treatment is indicated in the convalescence period and for the treatment of sequelae.

1) Filiform needle needling

a. Point selection

The points can be selected mainly from the Hand- or Foot-Yangming Meridians. Generally several groups of points are used alternately.

For paralysis of the upper limb: Dazhui (DU 14), Jianyu (LI 15), Quchi (LI 11), Shousanli (LI 10), Waiguan (SJ 9), supported by Jianliao (SJ 14), Jianzhen (SI 9), Huatuojiaji Points C_{5-7}

For paralysis of the lower limb: Mingmen (DU 4), Huantiao (GB 30), Biguan (ST 31), Futu (LI 18), Fengshi (GB 20), Yinmen (BL 37), Zusanli (ST 36), Yanglingquan (SP 9), Huatuojiaji Points L_{1-5}, supported by Zhibian (BL 54), Weizhong (BL 40), Kunlun (BL 60), Xuanzhong (GB 39), Jiexi (ST 41)

For paralysis of the muscles in the neck, back and waist: Fengchi (GB 20), Tianzhu (BL 10), Dazhu (BL 11), Qihaishu (BL 24), Shenshu (BL 23), Shangliao (BL 31) and Huatuojiaji Points

For paralysis of the abdominal muscles: Zhongwan (RN 12), Tianshu (ST 25), Guanyuan (RN 4), Qihai (RN 6)

b. Manipulation

Immediate needling should be performed when paralysis first appears with "shallow needling with multiple needles", such as twirling bird-peck needling for 10 seconds to 1 minute. No retaining of needle is needed. For excess syndrome, reducing method is adopted while for deficiency syndrome, reinforcing method is adopted. Deep insertion with moderate simulation is often used to treat the long-standing cases. Retain the needle for 15 to 30 minutes, during which the needle should be manipulated for 2 to 3 times.

c. Therapeutic course

The treatment is given once daily or every other day. One month is considered as a therapeutic course. An interval between two courses is 20 days.

2) Needling with big needles

a. Point selection

Changqiang (DU 1), Mingmen (DU 4), Zhiyang (DU 9)

First insert the needle from Changqiang up to Mingmen. Then insert the second needle from Mingmen up to Zhiyang and insert the third needle from Zhiyang up to Dazhui (DU 14). This is known as "three needles at the back".

Adjunct points:

For paralysis of the upper limb: from Jianyu (LI 15), to Quchi (LI 11), from Waiguan (SJ 5) to Quchi (LI 11)

For paralysis of the lower limb: from Weizhong (BL 40), to Chengfu (BL 36)

For talipes valgus: from Neihuijian (medial malleolus tip) to Sanyinjiao (SP 6)

For talipes varus: from Waihuijian (lateral malleolus tip) to Guangming (GB 37)

For retroversion of the knee joint: from Zusanli (ST 36) to Xiyangguan (GB 33)

b. Manipulation

A 8-cun No. 26 needle is used to insert rapidly along the subcutaneous part. After insertion, level the needle shaft to have an angle of 15° to 30° to the skin. Push the needle quickly to the point which should be gone through. Keep the direction forward along the Du Meridian with no deviation. When the needle advances to a certain depth, lift and thrust it for 3 to 5 times. Then withdraw the needle until 0.5 cm of the needle remaining and manipulate it both rightward and leftward. The angle made between the needle and the spinal column should be 30°. The big needle is also used in the same way when the adjunct points are needled.

c. Therapeutic course

One treatment is given everyday. 10 treatments constitute one therapeutic course.

3) Oral acupuncture (Needling inside the mouth)

a. Point selection

Area for the upper limb: from the maxillary lateral incisor to the second molar and vestibular mucosa

Points for the upper arm: on the mucosa between the second bicuspid premolar and the first molar on the left side of the maxilla

Points for the forearm: on the mucosa between the cuspid and the first bicuspid premolar on the left side of the maxilla.

Area for the lower limb: from the mandibular inferior incisor to the third molar and vestibular mucosa

Points for the thigh: on the mucosa between the second bicuspid premolar and the first molar on the left side of the mandible and the inferior part of gum of the vestibular part

Points for the knee: on the mucosa between the first and second bicuspid premolars on the left side of the mandible and the inferior part of gum

Points for the leg: on the mucosa between the cuspid and the first bicuspid premolar on the left side of the mandible and the inferior part of gum

Points of the right side have the similar locations.

b. Manipulation

Perform oblique or level insertion to the point on the affected side with a No. 30 filiform needle. Retain the needle for 30 minutes. After insertion, should encourage the patient to move the affected limb.

c. Therapeutic course

Treatment is given once every other day. A therapeutic course consists of 10 treatments.

4) Point injection

Prescription 1

a. Point selection

The points which are 1 cun aside on both sides of C4 to T2 are selected for paralysis of the upper limb.

The points which are 1 cun aside on both sides of T12 to L5 are selected for paralysis of the lower limb.

b. Manipulation

In each treatment, two pairs of points are selected (2 on each side). The needle is inserted obliquely to the direction of the spinal column with an angle of 45°. After deqi, inject certain amount of Vit. B_1 and B_{12} mixture to the points respectively. Sometimes 1 to 2.5 mg of Galanthamine is added to the mixture.

c. Therapeutic course

One treatment every day or every other day. A therapeutic course consists of 10 treatments.

Prescription 2

a. Point selection

Yinmen (BL 37), Huantiao (GB 30), Futu (LI 8), Zusanli (ST 36)

b. Manipulation

Inject 3—5 ml of 10% Glucose or 1 ml of long-acting Vit. B_1 to each acupoint.

c. Therapeutic course

Same as above.

Prescription 3

a. Point selection

For paralysis of the upper limb: Jianyu (LI 15), Shousanli (LI 10), Sidu (SJ 9), supported by Waiguan (SJ 5), Neiguan

(PC 6), Yangchi (SJ 4), Zhongzhu (KI 15), Baxie (EX-UE 9) and Dazhui (DU 14)

For paralysis of the lower limb: Futu (LI 18), Zusanli (ST 36), Jianxi (3 cun above the mid-point of the upper margin of the patella), supported by Biguan (ST 31), Xuehai (SP 10), Chengfu (BL 36), Weizhong (BL 40), Zuwaifan (1 cun of the medial side of Chengshan), Zuneifan (1 cun of the lateral side of Chengshan) Genping (on the Achilles tendon of the line joining the medial and lateral malleolus), and Jiexi (ST 41)

b. Manipulation

In each treatment, 3—4 points are punctured and 0. 01 to 0. 03 mg of Scopolamine/kg body weight can be injected to each point respectively everyday.

c. Therapeutic course

One treatment is given once everyday. 30 treatments constitute one therapeutic course. A spacing of 7 to 10 days, if necessary, is arranged between two courses.

5) Needling with row needles

a. Point selection

Points or point groups are selected according to Jingluo Bian Zheng, that is, points are selected according to the disease site, Jingluo distribution and transmission routes of the meridians, combined by the distribution of the paralysed muscles and their functional states. Group 1 includes the points of the spleen-stomach meridians, Group II includes the points of the gallbladder-bladder meridian. These two point-groups are needled alternately daily. In each treatment, 2 to 3 points from Ren and Du meridians can also be selected as adjunct points.

b. Manipulation

Time of the treatment

According to the method of "Midnight-noon Ebb-flow", the treatment can be given on the two time periods —— CHEN, and SI (7 and 11 a. m.) when the qi and blood are most vigorous.

Therapeutic method

After the related meridian and points are determined, two

rows of needles are inserted in the given order on the lower limb, starting from the end of the injured part, and going up along the meridian. Then try to induce qi by manipulating each needle. After deqi, strengthen the stimulation mainly by lifting the needle with less thrusting and direct the needling sensation to transmit from the higher level downwards along the meridian until it reaches the diseased meridian and collateral. At last, connect the shafts of the needle to the pulse electric current apparatus with fine copper wire. Each treatment lasts 20 minutes with gradual increase in the intensity of electro-stimulation. For the first eight minutes, the sparse wave is used. From the 8th to 10th minute, dense sparse wave is given. And from the 10th minute up to 20th minute the continuous wave is used.

c. Therapeutic course

The treatment is given once everyday. 12 treatments constitute one therapeutic course. An interval of 7 days should be arranged between two courses. After 3 courses, there should be a rest of 6 months before next 3 courses.

6) Electrotherapy

a. Point selection

For paralysis of the upper limb: Jianzhen (SI 9), Binao (LI 14), Quchi (LI 11), Waiguan (SJ 5)

For paralysis of the lower limb: Huantiao (GB 30), Zhibian (BL 54), Yinlian (LR 11), Futu (LI 18), Weizhong (BL 40), Chengshan (BL 57), Yanglingquan (GB 34), Zusanli (ST 36).

These points can be needled in pairs. In each treatment, 2 to 3 pairs can be selected.

b. Manipulation

After the insertion, try to make the needle sensation transmit to the distal end of the limbs. Then connect the needle with a G-6805 stimulator and strengthen the stimulation progressively until the muscles concerned contracts with a rhythm same to the needling frequency. Maintain the treatment for half a minute, and after a while, repeat the treatment for another half a minute. Repetition is carried on for 3 to 4 times.

c. Therapeutic course

One treatment is given once every other day. 10 treatments constitute one therapeutic course.

7) Skin needling

a. Point selection

For paralysis of the upper limb: Back neck, chest, shoulder, the affected limb. Tap mainly both sides of the thoracic vertebrae 1—4, the affected limb, as well as Quchi (LI 11), Waiguan (SJ 5) and the finger tips.

For paralysis of the lower limb: Waist, sacral area, affected limb. Meanwhile. tap along the transmission routes of the Stomach Meridian of the Foot-Yangming, the Spleen Meridian of the Foot-Taiyin, and the Liver Meridian of the Foot Jueyin. Tap mainly both sides of the lumbar vertebrae 4—5 and such points as Zusanli (ST 36), Yinlingquan (SP 9), Jiexi (ST 41), and Huantiao (GB 30).

When the symptoms are basically improved, tap both sides of the spinal column, especially the T_{5-12} and the waist. Slightly needle the affected limb.

b. Manipulation

Perform light stimulation (skin slight reddish) or moderate stimulation (skin reddish but no bleeding). Tap teh affected limb everyday, and the healthy limb every other day.

c. Therapeutic course

Same as above.

8) Moxibustion

a. Point selection

Same as those in Filiform needle needling

b. Manipulation

Perform warm moxibustion on 3 to 4 main points in each treatment. Each point is moxibustioned for 5 to 10 minutes until skin becomes reddish and there is slight sweating.

c. Therapeutic course

Same as above.

9) Point catgut implantation

a. Point selection

Mainly from the Hand- or Foot-Yangming Meridians, supported by the paralysed muscle group. In each treatment, take the yang meridian first, then the yin meridian. The points on upper part of the limb first, then those on the lower part. When there is myotrophy and joint deformity, treat the myotrophy first, then joint deformity. When the paralysis involves more than one limb, treat the lightly-affected limb first, then the severely-affected limb. For paralysis of the upper limb, Dazhui (DU 14), Jianyu (LI 15), Quchi (LI 11), and Waiguan (SJ 5) are often selected. For paralysis of the lower limb, Mingmen (DU 4), Huantiao (GB 30), Maibu (2 cun below point Biguan) and Zusanli (ST 36) are often taken. In each treatment, 3 to 5 points are needled.

b. Manipulation

Catgut implantation with a triangle-needle

Under local anesthesia (1.5 to 3 cm on both sides of the point), insert the triangle-needle with catgut into the skin from one side of the point, push the needle, through the point, out through the other side. Pull the catgut to and fro to produce a numbness-distension sensation. Then cut off the catgut close to the skin and cover the needle holes with gauze. Try to remain the catgut in the body as long as possible and not to expose the catgut ends. This method is suitable to most of the superficial points.

Catgut implantation with puncture needles

Put 1 to 2 cm catgut in the anterior part of a puncture needle (with leveled tip). Cut the skin of the point, then insert the puncture needle into the point. Massage the skin to produce numbness-distension sensation. Then implant the catgut into the point. This method is suitable for some deep points such as Huantiao.

Catgut ligation therapy

Under local anesthesia at 1.5 to 2.5 cm by the side of the selected point, and cut the skin at a site vertical to the transmission route of the Jingluo for 3 to 5 mm long, then insert a blood vessel clamp through the incision obliquely to the sensitive spot in the muscles. After deqi or the needling sensation occurs, withdraw the clamp and insert a large triangle-needle with catgut through the incision. Make it penetrate the shallow part of the sensitive spot and get out of the skin from the original incision. Tie the catgut and implant it into the deep part of the incision. There is no need to suture the wound, and just cover it with gauze. (Fig. 1)

c. Therapeutic course

This treatment can be given once a month.

Therapeutic Effect

1) Acupuncture can be used respectively in the early stage of paralysis, restoration stage and the stage when the sequelae appear. The therapeutic effect is better for those patients with younger age, and mild disease with short duration.

Dr. Lu Xingzhai treated 212 cases with filiform needle needling, among whom 49.5% were cured with a total effective reate of 96.2%. (Journal of Henan TCM, 1984; 6)

Dr. Guo Zhuan treated 310 cases with disease duration varying from 8 days to 2 years and reported 50.9% was cured and 35.5% remarkably improved. The total effective rate reached 99.1%. (Journal of Henan TCM, 1984; 5)

2) It is generally considered that a combined method is better than a single needling method in treating the disease. Therefore, several different therapeutic methods can be used in combination so as to raise the therapeutic effect.

3) The therapeutic effect can be enhanced by limb exercises, massage, ... etc.

4) Surgical operation should be performed if there is joint deformity.

Discussion

1) In recent year, the disease has become very rare with the

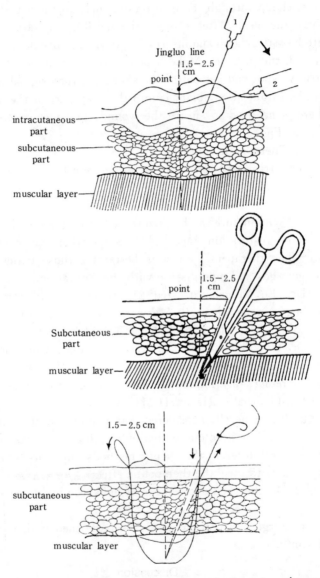

Fig. 1 The sketch map for point-stimulation and point suture therapy

use of live poliomyelitis vaccine.

2) There are 1% to 1‰ of the patients with myoatrophy or paralysis after the disease, therefore the acupuncture still plays an important role in treatment.

3) Dr. Wang Qide holds that the key point in treating the disease is "to select points from Sanguan". (The so-called "Sanguan" refers to shoulder joint, elbow joint and wrist joint in upper limb, and waist/hip joint, knee joint and ankle joint in lower limb. The Shu points on or close to the joints should be needled in the treatment.) In treating paralysis of the lower limb, (either from the left limb or the right limb) Shenshu (both sides), Mingmen and Dachangshu (both sides) should be needled in each treatment without retaining of needles. Cupping therapy should then be applied until bleeding occurs from the point. In treating paralysis of the upper limb, Dazhui should be needled in each treatment, supported by the points on local joint or close to the joint which can be used alternately. In each treatment 3 to 4 points from each joint can be selected. The manipulation consists of large amplitude twirling, rotating and lifting-thrusting. In the late stage of the treatment, the reducing method should be replaced by reinforcing method and the number of points to be needled should also be lessened. Cupping therapy should then be performed. From needling to cupping, point radiation with ultra-red ray should be performed in the whole process. (Journal of Chinese Acupuncture, 1985; 6)

4) In treating paralysis of the upper limb:

Dr. Jia Guangtian took Jianyu (LI 15), Jianliao (SJ 14), Quchi (LI 11), Shousanli (LI 10), Hegu (LI 4), and Yaoshu (DU 2) as the main points. When there is difficulty in raising the shoulder, Tianzhong (SI 11) and Binao (LI 14) are added. If there is weakness in stretching the arm, Bizhong, Neiguan (PC 6) and Waiguan (SJ 5) are added. When there is eversion or inversion of hand, Yangchi (SJ 4), Yangxi (LI 5), Houxi (SI 3), Sidu (SJ 9) and Shaohai (HT 3) are added. For wrist drop, Waiguan and Sidu are added. The needling is often supported by the method of electric-shock-like needling on Futu (LI 18) (bird-pecking after the slow insertion. Twirling the needle in large amplitude can produce electric-shock sensation referring to the tips of the fingers.).

In treating paralysis of the lower limb, Shenshu (BL 23), Dazhui (DU 14), Mingmen (DU 4), Huantiao (GB 30), Baliao, Yinmen (BL 37), Liangqiu (ST 34), Weizhong (BL 40), Yanglingquan (GB 34) and Jiexi (ST 41) are selected as the main points. For difficulty in raising the leg, Biguan (ST 31) is added. For difficulty in flexing the knee, Yinshi (ST 33), Chengshan (BL 57), and Kunlun (BL 60) are added. For foot inversion, Fengshi (GB 31), Qiuxu (GB 40) and Xuanzhong (GB 39) are added. For foot eversion, Yinlingquan (SP 9) and Neiting (ST 44) are added. For talipes equinus, Futu (LI 18), Zusanli (ST 36) and Neiting are added. After pricking method is used, let out the stagnant blood with the method of cupping. In treating those who walks with the hand placing on the knee, four bamboo splints are used to wrap tightly around the affected knee. Then needling is conducted on Zhibian (BL 54) to have an electric current-like sensation transmit to the tips of the toes, or until there is muscle-shaking. Meanwhile, cupping and red-hot needle needling are used to support the treatment. (Journal of Chinese Acupuncture, 1987; 4:7)

2. Syringomyelia

Syringomyelia is a chronic progressive disease characterized by disappearance of sensory sensation, muscular atrophy and weakness of the limbs which are caused by the cavitation in the central part of the spinal cord. These symptoms are also complicated by nutritive disturbance. The etiology of the disease is unknown. As it is often complicated by congenital deformity, it is often related to the congenital dysplasia. The cavity is often located at the lower cervical section of the spinal cord with various length. The expansion of the cavity may injure the motor/sensory nerve track and the cells of the anterior and posterior and the lateral horns. For the disease there is still no effective treatment.

The disease develops slowly. After the treatment, some symptoms may be improved, and in some cases, it may remain unchanged for years.

According to TCM, this disease belongs to the category of "arthralgia syndrome", "numbness" and "flaccidity syndrome".

Clinical Manifestation

1) The disease starts most often when the patients are at the age between 20 to 30 years old, though some cases were found among the school children and the teenages. The incidence rate among the males is slightly higher than that among the females.

2) The distribution of the earliest symptoms are of a segmental nature. They will vary according to the area of the spinal cross-section that is involved. The symptoms appear most often in the upper limbs.

3) Sensory disturbance: Segmental pain and disturbance of temperature sensation often occur in the ulnar side of arm and hand and upper part of the chest in the diseased side, but nothing abnormal (or relatively normal) is found for touching and deep sensation. There may also be symmetric segmental dissociative sensory disorder and segmental complete sensory disorder in some cases. The area with sensory disturbance is often scalded, burned by hot subject and with painless ulcer.

4) Motor and reflex disturbance: Muscular atrophy and weakness are found in the upper limb (The thenar and interosseous muscles are first but most seriously affected.) The affected muscles may show tremor, and the tendon reflex decreased or disappeared. When the pyramidal tract is injured, there is spastic paralysis in the lower limbs with hypermyotonia, abdominal reflex decreased or disappeared and tendon reflex hyperactive. The asymmetrical atrophy and weakness of the muscles on each side of the back may result in scoliosis.

5) Nutritive disturbance: Often manifest as muscular atro-

phy, thickened skin, cyanosis, profuse or no sweating, parony-chia, limited atrophy of the subcutaneous tissues, bullous skin rash and blue-black pigmentation at the ends of the limbs. Those with the disease on the lateral horn of the cervical part may have Horner's syndrome (enophthalmos, miosis, blepharoptosis and facial hypohidrosis on the affected side). In most cases, new or old burn -like scars and intractable ulcer can be noted at the limb ends of the segmental analgesia site. There may be deformity of the fingers or toes, painless necrosis and loss of the last knuckle or even all fingers. There is joint damage in about 25% to 30% of the patients, which is more commonly seen in the upper limbs.

6) When the cavity develops deeper into the medullary bulb, there will be facial sensory disturbance, nystagmus, dysphagia, dysphonia, atrophy of the tongue muscle complicated by tongue twitching, uranoplegia and atrophy of sternocleidomastoid and trapezius muscle.

7) Generally, examination of the cerebrospinal fluid reveals normal findings, but in some cases, the protein may increased slightly. In the late stage of the disease, there are a few cases who have obstruction of the vertebral canal with increased pro-teins. The X-ray film of the skull and the spinal column may show congenital dysostosis; the myelography may show com-pression or broadening of the spinal cord; and the radionuclide scanning can define the range of the cavity or the kinetic changes of the cerebrospinal fluid.

Acupuncture Treatment

The acupuncture treatment can be applied according to the symptoms.

1) Filiform needle needling

a. Point selection

Huatuojiaji points (EX-B 2), Fuliu (KI 7), Jianyu (LI 15), Quchi (LI 11), Shousanli (LI 10), Waiguan (SJ 5), Hegu (LI 4), Yuji (LU 10), Baxie (EX-UE 9), Huantiao (GB 30),

Biguan (ST 31), Futu (ST 32), Xuehai (SP 10), Liangqiu (ST 34), Zusanli (ST 36), Yanglingquan (GB 34), Jiexi (ST 41), Juegu (GB 30), Bafeng (EX-LE 10)

These points can be supported by such adjunct points as Tainzong (SI 11), Jianliao (SJ 14), Shaohai (HT 3), Xiaohai (SI 8), Zhongwan (RN 12), Qihai (RN 6), Guanyuan (RN 4) and the Shu points close to the affected area.

b. Manipulation

Mainly the reinforcing method by lifting-thrusting and twirling-rotating should be performed. After deqi, the needles can be connected with a G-6805 stimulator for 15 minutes or moxibustion with moxa sticks.

c. Therapeutic course

The treatment is given once every other day. 10 treatments constitute one therapeutic course.

2) Scalp acupuncture

a. Point selection

Dingzhongxian, Upper 1/5 and 2/5 of Dingnie Qianxiexian, Upper 1/5 and 2/5 of Dingnie Houxiexian, Zhenshang Zhenzhongxian and Zhenshang Pangxian

b. Manipulation

"Qi withdrawal"is used for all the points except Dingzhongxian on which qi entering is used. Retain the needle for 2 to 48 hours during which the needles are manipulated for 3 to 5 times.

c. Therapeutic course

The treatment is given once every other day. 10 treatments constitute one therapeutic course.

d. Exercises

The patients should concentrate their minds on the affected part and conduct the active or passive movement during treatment. The time of exercises should be no less than 2 hours everyday, until slight sweating all over the body.

3) Skin acupuncture

a. Point selection

Both sides of the spinal column and the affected part

Blood letting is conducted once every three days on the finger (toe) tips of the affected limb.

b. Manipulation

Needling with moderate or slightly heavy stimulation until the local skin becomes reddish with no bleeding or light bleeding. Multiple needlings or called dense needling should be applied on the affected part.

c. Therapeutic course

The treatment is given once every other day. 10 treatments constitute one therapeutic course.

Therapeutic Effect

1) By acupuncture there is symptomatic improvements including decrease in the area with sensory disturbance.

2) According to China's Plum-Blossom Needle, this therapeutic method offers a rather good effect for this illness. After 5 treatments, there were more sweating on the affected side and less pain in the fingers than before. After 35 treatments, the symptoms became further improved with more sweating. After 80 treatments, there was no pain in the fingers and the numbness in the affected side was attenuated. After 122 treatments, both the pain and the numbness were disappeared. After 141 treatments, the patient was cured completely with no uncomfortable feelings. A follow-up of over one year showed that the therapeutic result is satisfactory.

Discussion

1) According to TCM differentiation, this disease is closely related to insufficient qi and blood, and is concerned very much with the disease of the liver, kidneys or lungs. During the acupuncture treatment, the most important thing is to remove obstruction in the meridians to relieve pain, to warm the meridians and collaterals, and to regulate qi and blood. Therefore, a combined way, such as filiform needle needling with scalp acupuncture, point injection with Vit. B group, warm moxibus-

tion, skin needling, point irradiation with ultra-red ray ... can be applied to relieve the symptoms.

2) Burn and frostbite should be prevented for those with analgesia.

3) During the acupuncture treatment, passive limb movement such as massage should be practiced to accelerate the recovery.

3. Injury of Brachial Plexus

Consisting of the anterior branches of the fifth to eighth cervical nerves and most of the anterior branches of the first pair of the thoracic nerves, the brachial plexus locates at the posterosuperior part of the subclavian artery, through the scalene muscle interstice and the posterior part of the clavicle to the armpit, where it forms three bundles surrounding the axillary artery. That located in the medial side of the axillary artery is called medial fasciculus, that in the lateral side is lateral fasciculus and that in the posterior part is posterior fasciculus. Injury of brachial plexus can lead to the motor and sensory disturbance of the upper limb and the shoulder.

Clinical Manifestation

1) There is the history of trauma or birth trauma.

2) There is paralysis of the upper limb and motor disturbance of the shoulder in the affected sides. In severe cases, there will be paralysis of the muscle pectoralis major and minor and serratus anterior.

3) Except the upper part of the deltoid muscle and the medial side of the upper arm, the sensation of upper limb disappears totally.

Acupuncture Treatment

1) Filiform needle needling
a. Point selection
Huatuojiaji (EX-B 2) C5 to T1, Jianjing (GB 21), Jianyu

(LI 15), Jianzhen (SI 9), Jianneiling, Jianwailing, Quchi (LI 11), Waiguan (SJ 5), Hegu (LI 4) and Houxi (SI 3)

b. Manipulation

Huatuojiaji points from both sides or the affected side are needled perpendicularly with the No. 26—28 filiform needles (1.5 to 2 cun long) to 1 to 1.5 cun deep. Uniform reinforcing and reducing method are performed. 3 to 4 points in the limb can be selected in each treatment and lifting-thrusting and twirling-rotating in large amplitude is adopted to produce electric-shock sensation and involuntary limb movement.

c. Therapeutic course

One to two treatments daily. A therapeutic course consists of 10 treatments. There should be an interval of 7 to 10 days between two courses.

2) Electric therapy

a. Point selection

Same as those in Filiform needle needling.

b. Manipulation

In each treatment, 2 to 4 points are taken. After deqi, connect the needles with a G-6805 stimulator with gradual increasing frequency. Each treatment lasts about 15 to 20 minutes.

c. Therapeutic course

The treatment is given once every other day. 10 treatments constitute one therapeutic course.

3) Point injection

a. Point selection

Same as Filiform needle needling.

b. Manipulation

Make a mixture of 20 mg. of Vit. B_1, 0.1 mg. of Vit. B_{12} and 1 mg. of Galanthamine. After deqi, inject 0.5 to 1 ml. of the mixture into each of the two points selected in each treatment.

c. Therapeutic course

The treatment is given once everyday. 10 treatmemts constitute one therapeutic course.

4) Scalp acupuncture

a. Point selection

Middle 2/3 of Dingnie Qianxiexian (the healthy side), Ding-pangxian II (the healthy side) and Dingnie Houxian [from Lu-oque (BL 8) to Baihui (DU 20)]

b. Manipulation

Insert a No. 30 (1.5 cun long) needle swiftly into the lower part of the aponeurosis and perform reducing with "qi withdraw-al". Retain the needle for 2 to 24 hours. During needling and retaining of needle, limb exercises should be practiced.

c. Therapeutic course

The treatment is given once every other day. 10 treatments constitute one therapeutic course.

d. Exercises

In needling Dingnie Qianxiexian and Dingpangxian II, the patient should concentrate his mind on the paralysed upper limb. Both active and passive movement are encouraged. When Ding-nie Houxian is needled, the patient should focus his mind on the affected part of the shoulder. The passive and active shoulder movement should be practiced. During retaining of needle, the shoulder movement should be conducted for no less than 2 hours everyday.

Therapeutic Effect

1) Those with brachial plexus injury should be treated ener-getically within 3 months after the injury. Especially those that belong to closed injury should be needled as early as possible so as to restore the damaged functions and to lessen the complica-tions.

2) Dr. Ma Zhiui once treated a case of paralysis of the brachial plexus caused by stone-hitting. The patient suffered al-so from muscular atrophy. Dr. Ma mixed Vit. B_1 200 mg. and Vit. B_{12} 0.5 mg., and injected 1.5 ml. of the mixture into the following points — Jianjing (GB 21), Jiansanzhen (3 points on the shoulder), Hongzhong, Waiguan (SJ 5), Taijian, Jubi,

Nerve roots of the left side of L5 and L6, Jianhou, Naoshu (SJ 10) and Jianliao (SJ 14). (In each treatment, 4 points were taken.) During the treatment, functional exercises were suggested. Such therapeutic methods as electric needling, filiform needle needling were also performed. The patient was completely cured after 10 therapeutic courses. (Journal of Shanghai Acupuncture, 1986; 3:5)

3) Acupuncture is not effective in case of complete severing of the nerve.

4. Brachial Plexus Neuritis

This disease often follows a epidemic influenza, or the inflammation of the nearby tissues and various kind of infections. The symptoms include pain in the area controlled by branchial plexus and weakness or atrophy of the related muscles.

This disease belongs to "arthralgia-syndrome" in TCM.

Clinical Manifestation

1) With acute onset, the disease is more commonly seen in adult patients who have had a history of epidemic influenza or inflammations.

2) Pain often occurs in the root of the neck and the upper part of the clavicular region and may occur on the back of shoulders, arm, forearm and hand. The pain becomes more severe when the arm is abducted or raised. There is also apparent tenderness at the upper and lower clavicle pits or the armpit. The pain, at first, is intermittent burning, pricking, or sore in character. After some time it becomes continuous with paroxysmal aggravation.

3) There will be weakness, paralysis or atrophy of the muscles controlled by the brachial plexus.

Acupuncture Treatment

1) Filiform needle needling
a. Point selection

Jingbi, which can be taken in dorsal position, is a point on 1 cun above the junction of the inner 1/3 and outer 2/3 of the clavicle.

Adjunct points: When there is pain radiating to the radial side, Quchi (LI 11) is added, and when to ulnar side, Xiaohai (SI 8) is added. For severe pain in the proximal end and the shoulder, Jianneiling is added.

b. Manipulation

When Jingbi is needled, insert the needle perpendicularly to 0.5 — 0.8 cun (Note: no oblique insertion or deep insertion). When Jianneiling is needled, make penetration needling of 1 to 1.5 cun to the direction of the back of the shoulder. After deqi, electric stimulation can be applied with a frequency of 123 times/minute for 30 to 60 minutes.

c. Therapeutic course

One treatment is given everyday. 10 treatments constitute one therapeutic course.

2) Scalp acupuncture

a. Point selection

Dingnie Houxian (the opposite side of the focus), Middle 2/5 of Dingnie Qianxiexian (the opposits side of the focus), Middle 2/5 of Dingnie Houxiexian (the opposite side of the focus) and Dingzhongxian.

b. Manipulation

When the needle is inserted to the lower part of the aponeurosis, "qi withdrawal" should be performed. Retain the needle for 24 hours.

c. Therapeutic course

One treatment is given everyday. 5 to 7 treatments are made up of one therapeutic course.

d. Exercises

During needling and retaining of needle, try to move the affected limb properly.

3) Needle warming through moxibustion

a. Point selection

Huatuojiaji C_5 and C_6, Jianjing (GB 21), Naoshu (SJ 10), Jianliao (SJ 14), Jianneiling, Jianwailing, Waiguan (SJ 5), Jugu (LI 16)

b. Manipulation

After deqi with filiform needle, retain the needle and cast a moxa stick of 2 cm long on the needle body. The stick is about 2 to 3 cm apart from the skin. Burn the moxa stick from the lower end. (Note: Don't injure the skin by the falling ashes.)

c. Therapeutic course

One treatment is given every other day. 10 treatments are made up of one therapeutic course.

Therapeutic Effect

1) Acupuncture is effective in relieving inflammation and pain, and in restoring the myodynamia. Dr. Xi Zhongzhi had treated 20 cases of branchial plexus neuritis with satisfactory results: 16 cases cured; 3 cases much improved and only one case failed. (Journal of Jiangsu TCM, 1985; 2) Generally a treatment of 6 to 8 months can cure the patients of their disease.

2) Needle warming through moxibustion is very effective for the paralysis and muscular atrophy caused by brachial plexus neuritis. The therapeutic effect can be raised if functional exercises are practiced to support the treatment.

3) When this disease is treated with acupuncture the etiological treatment should be carried out simultaneously.

4) As this disease is secondary to cervical spondylopathy, in the treatment both diseases should be considered.

SECTION V
Paralysis of Individual Muscle Group

The paralysis of a certain muscle group, in most cases, is caused by the injury in the nerve root or the peripheral nerve stem that dominates this particular muscle group. Clinically the injury of the peripheral nerve is divided into two kinds — closed injury and open injury. The former often results from long-standing local compression, and stretching, contusion as well as irritating drugs. Generally the nerve is not severed completely. The latter is mainly caused by direct injury to the nerves by pointed or sharp subjects or weapons. Sometimes, the nerve can be severed completely. Infection of peripheral nerve or inflammation of nearby tissues can also lead to paralysis on the muscles innervated by the involved nerve.

1. Radial Nerve Injury

The radial nerve is the most vulnerable nerve among all the nerves in brachial plexus. As the upper section of this nerve is located very close to the radial groove which is on the dorsal part of the middle section of humerus, it is very easy to be injured when there is humeral fracture. In addition, using the arm as pillow during sleep, and long time abduction of the upper limb during an operation, may also cause injury of that nerve. In TCM, it belongs to the category of "flaccidity syndrome".

Clinical Manifestation

1) The patient may have a history of humeral fracture or injury of the upper limbs.

2) There is paralysis of the extensor muscle and the supina-

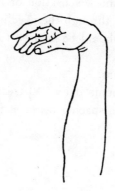

Fig. 2 "Wrist drop" in radial nerve injury

tor muscle. There is also rigidity of the elbow, wrist and metacarpophalangeal joints. The forearm often fails to make supination.

3) In raising the forearm, there is "wrist drop". (Fig. 2)

4) The disappearance of sensory sensation occurs most apparently in the area between the first and the second metacarpal bones on the back of the hand.

Acupuncture Treatment

1) Filiform needle needling

Prescription 1

a. Point selection

Huatuojiaji points (EX-B 2) C_5-T_1, Jiquan (HT 1), Jianyu (LI 15), Binao (LI 14), Chize (LU 5), Quchi (LI 11), Shousanli (LI 10), Pianli (LI 6), Hegu (LI 4)

b. Manipulation

Huatuojiaji points (either from the affected side or from both sides) can be needled perpendicularly to 1 — 1 . 5 cun and uniform reinforcing or reducing method is often adopted. 3 to 4 points on the limbs can be taken in each treatment, with maneuver of lifting-thrusting and twirling-rotating in large amplitude. Reducing for those with pain and reinforcing for those with paralysis. An electric shock sensation or involuntary spasmodic jerks should be induced through the needling. The patients with impairment of motion should be advised to exercise the affected limb.

c. Therapeutic course

One to two treatments daily. 10 treatments constitute one therapeutic course. The spacing between two courses is 7 to 10 days.

Prescription 2

a. Point selection

Jingbi, Jiquan (HT 1), Shousanli (LI 10), Quchi (LI 11),

from Hegu (LI 4) to Houxi (SI 3)

b. Manipulation

In needling point Jingbi, ask the patient to lie in a lateral recumbent position and insert the needle horizontally into the point slowly by twirling for 0. 3 to 0. 8 cun. Make the soreness, numbness or electric shock sensation transmit to the fingers. The downward oblique insertion must be avoided. All the other points should be needled with reducing method.

c. Therapeutic course

One treatment daily. 10 treatments constitute one therapeutic course.

2) Needling with thick needle

a. Point selection

Shousanli (LI 10), or needle the radial nerve.

b. Manipulation

Needle Shousanli or the radial nerve with a needle which is about 90 mm long and with a diameter of 0. 6 mm. Strong stimulation should be induced and no retaining of needle is needed.

c. Therapeutic course

One treatment daily. 10 treatments constitute one therapeutic course.

3) Electric therapy

a. Point selection

Jianzhen (SI 9), Quchi (LI 11); Shousanli (LI 10), Hegu (LI 4)

b. Manipulation

The above two groups of points can be needled alternately. After deqi, with a filiform needle, connect the needle with a G-6805 stimulator (connect the needles in Jianzhen and Shousanli with the cathode, and in Quchi and Hegu with anode). The frequency is 20 to 30 times/minute with ever-increasing quantity. A specific movement of wrist-raising should be induced. Each needling should last for 20 to 30 minutes.

c. Therapeutic course

One treatment is given every other day. 10 treatments constitute one therapeutic course. The spacing between two courses is 3 to 5 days.

4) Point injection

a. Point selection

Same as above.

b. Manipulation

In each treatment, 2 points are taken. To each point inject 0. 5 to 1 ml of the mixture containing 20 mg of Vit. B_1, 0. 1 mg of Vit. B_{12} and 1 mg of Galanthamine.

c. Therapeutic course

One treatment is given everyday. 10 treatments constitute one therapeutic course.

5) Scalp acupuncture

a. Point selection

Dingzhongxian, Middle 2/5 of the Dingnie Qianxiexian (healthy side). Add Middle 2/5 of the Dingnie Houxiexian for those with muscular pain.

b. Manipulation

Perform "qi withdrawal" after the needle enters the lower part of the galea aponeurotica. Retain the needle for 24 hours. Exercises of the affected limb should be conducted in the period of acupuncture.

c. Therapeutic course

One treatment is given every other day. 10 treatments constitute one therapeutic course.

d. Exercises

Active or passive movements such as flexion and extension of the elbow, wrist and metacarpophalangeal joints, supination of the forearm and wrist-raising should be practiced by the patient. In addition, nassage and rubbing of the affected areas may also help raise the therapeutic effect.

Therapeutic Effect

Early treatment will ensure a satisfactory therapeutic result. Needling may help restore the functions of the affected area and lessen the sequelae.

Dr. Luo Guoli treated 30 cases of radical nerve injury with satisfactory results: 18 cases cured; 3 cases with excellent therapeutic effect; 8 cases improved, and 1 case with no effect. (Journal of Shanxi TCM, 1983; 12)

Dr. Yang Yuquan treated 44 cases of peripheral nerve injury mainly with electric therapy, and found that the best result is seen in cases of paralysis caused by radical nerve injury. (Journal of Shanghai Acupuncture, 1983; 2)

2. Common Peroneal Nerve Injury

The common peroneal nerve is one of the main branches of the sciatic nerve. It can be injured by trauma, crush, fracture or ischemia and inflammation in the upper part of the fibula. In TCM, it belongs to the category of "flaccidity syndrome".

Clinical Manifestation

1) Many factors can cause injury of the common peroneal nerve, such as improper sleeping, pathogenic cold or a common cold, or compression of the peroneal nerve by tight bandage or plaster bandage on the leg below the head of fibula.

2) The onset of disease is usually sudden.

3) The patient can not stretch the foot, raise the foot and toes, and made foot abduction or pronation because of paralysis of the peroneal muscle and the anterior tibial muscles.

4) There are foot drop and flexion of the first section of toe. In a long-standing disease, there will be typical talipes equinovarus.

5) There are sensory disturbance in the anterolateral aspect of the leg and the back of foot, and muscular atrophy in the anterolateral part of the leg. The Achilles tendon reflex is normal.

Acupuncture Treatment

1) Filiform needle needling
a. Point selection

Huatuojiaji (EX-B 2) L_4-L_5, Yinmen (BL 37), Weiyang (BL 39), Yanglingquan (GB 34), Zulinqi (GB 41); Huantiao (GB 30), Zusanli (ST 36), Yanglingquan, Jiexi (ST 41), Taichong (LR 3)

b. Manipulation

The above two groups of points can be selected at random. Huatuojiaji from the affected side or from both sides can be needled perpendicularly for 2 to 3 cun. Try to induce an electric shock sensation by lifting-thrusting and twirling-rotating in large amplitude. Except Zusanli and Jiexi, all the points should be manipulated with reducing method. After deqi, retain the needle for 30 minutes, during which the needles can be manipulated once every ten minutes.

c. Therapeutic course

One treatment is given everyday. 10 treatments constitute one therapeutic course. The spacing between two courses is 3 to 5 days.

2) Elongated needle needling

a. Point selection

Sanjian, Sanyang, Sanling, Guangming (GB 37), Jiexi (ST 41), Qiuxu (GB 40)

b. Manipulation

Sanjian (three points: Jianbu — 2 cun aside of the lateral aspect of Chengfu; Jianzhong — 2 cun aside of the lateral aspect of Yinmen; Jianxia — 2 cun aside of the lateral aspect of 2 cun below Yinmen) are needled perpendicularly to the direction of sciatic nerve when the patient lies in the lateral recumbent and knee-flex position. The needling depth is about 3 to 4 cun. Make the numbness-electric shock sensation transmit up to the arm or down to the foot.

Sanyang includes 3 points related to Yanglingquan: (a) Yanglingquan itself; (b) a point 2 cun directly below Yanglingquan; (c) a point 4 cun directly below Yanglingquan. When these 3 points are needled, insert the needle obliquely from the posterior border of the tibia to about 1 to 3 cun. Make the soreness, numbness and distension sensation transmit to the foot.

Sanling also includes 3 points, of which the first one located 1 cun posterior to the head of fibula, and the other two are 2 cun and 4 cun right downward below the first one. When these points are needled, direct the needle obliquely to the medial aspect of tibia with a depth of about 2 to 3 cun. Make the soreness, numbness and distension sensation transmit to the lower limb.

Reducing will be performed when the rest points are needled.

c. Therapeutic course

One treatment is given everyday. 10 treatments constitute one therapeutic course. The spacing between two courses is one week.

3) Electric therapy

a. Point selection

Zusanli (ST 36), Yanglingquan (GB 34), Huantiao (GB 30), Weiyang (BL 39), Xuanzhong (GB 39), Jiexi (ST 41)

b. Manipulation

After deqi with needling, connect the needle to a G-6805 stimulator. A dense-sparse wave is selected and try to induce an obvious contraction in the affected muscles. In each treatment, 2 to 4 points are needled for 10 to 15 minutes.

c. Therapeutic course

One treatment is given everyday. 10 treatments constitute one therapeutic course. The spacing between two courses is 5 days.

4) Point injection

a. Point selection

Same as the Electric therapy.

b. Manipulation

Make a mixture of Vit. B_1 100 mg. , Vit. B_{12} 0.5 mg and 1 to 3 mg Galantamine. After deqi, inject the drug into the points. In each treatment, 3 points are injected. The points can be used in turn.

c. Therapeutic course

One treatment is given every other day. 10 treatments constitute one therapeutic course. The spacing between two courses is 5 days.

5) Skin needling

a. Point selection

Dazhui (DU 14), Mingmen (DU 4), Changqiang (DU 1), Feishu (BL 13), Geshu (BL 17), Pishu (BL 20), Baliao.

b. Manipulation

According to Bianzheng Lunzhi, syndrome of blood stasis type should be treated by heavily tapping Changqiang and lightly tapping Geshu. Syndrome of cold-dampness type is treated by heavily tapping Mingmen and Baliao. Syndrome of damp-heat type is treated by lightly tapping Feishu and Pishu, and heavily tapping Dazhui. For lightly tapping, the skin should be made flare and for heavily tapping, there should be slight bleeding on the local skin. The tapping can also be made along the Du Meridian on the back and on the Shu points of the Gallbladder Meridian of the Foot-Taiyang. Each point should be tapped for 60 to 80 times.

c. Therapeutic course

One treatment is given everyday. 10 treatments constitute one therapeutic course.

The treatment can also be performed in combination with Filiform needle needling.

6) Scalp acupuncture

a. Point selection

Dingzhongxian, Upper 1/5 of Dingnie Qianxiexian

b. Manipulation

After the needle enters the galea aponeurotica, level the needle and perform "qi withdrawal". During the needling, limb exercises should also be conducted. When Upper 1/5 of Dingnie Qianxiexian in the opposite side of the focus is needled, level needling is made along the Xiexian line. Meanwhile, penetration needling should be performed to the direction of Dingnie Houxiexian, and "qi withdrawal"is performed. Retain the needle for 24 hours.

c. Therapeutic course

One treatment is given every other day. 10 treatments constitute one therapeutic course.

d. Exercises

During needling and retaining of needle, the patient must concentrate his mind on the affected limb. Various kind of active or passive movements and massage or rubbing on the affected muscles should be performed. The time of exercises should be no less than 3 hours daily.

Therapeutic Effect

1) Acupuncture with filiform needle is very effective in the treatment or common peroneal nerve injury caused by trauma, ischemia or by pathogenic cold and fever. Dr. Xie Xianyuan had treated 40 cases and claimed that after a treatment of 7 to 12 times, all were cured. (Journal of TCM. 1982; 9)

2) According to the introduction of *Elongated Needle Needling*, a patient with common peroneal nerve injury had felt firmness in the affected lower limb and had had less difficulty in walking after a course of treatment with elongated needle needling. Then the patient was ordered to practice active functional exercises such as up-lifting of the ankle joint. He was completely cured after a continuous treatment of 3 months.

3) Dr. Zeng Shaojie once treated 36 cases of common peroneal nerve injury caused by intramuscular injection and the treatment consisted of electric therapy and point injection . The curative rate was 84.62% and the total effective rate was 100%. (Journal of Chinese Acupuncture, 1987; 4:7)

4) According to the differentiation, Dr. Yao Zunhua treated 52 cases of this disease with skin needling and filiform needle needling. As a result, 46 cases (88.5%) were cured, 4 cases (7.7%) were improved. 2 cases (3.8%) were with no effect. The total effective rate was 96.2%. The average treatment time

was 16.

5) The author also obtained very satisfactory therapeutic effect when he treated this disease with scalp acupuncture and filiform needle needling. It was found that the immediate therapeutic effect was excellent.

Discussion

1) The injury of the common peroneal nerve is very common clinically. The causes of this disease often include long-time squatting or genuflexion during working, invasion of pathogenic cold and dampness, trauma, injury due to intramuscular injection, as well as bone fracture, compression ... etc. Attention should be paid to the treatment according to the pathogenic causes. If necessary, acupuncture treatment can be applied.

2) A timely treatment is essential to ensure a better therapeutic effect. When muscular atrophy in a long-standing case is found, it is suggestive that the acupuncture should be combined with moxibustion so as to clear and activate the meridians and to promote the blood circulation.

3) Effort should be made to identify this disease from the paralysis caused by disease of the spinal cord, cerebrospinal accident, hypokalemia and poliomyelitis.

3. Peripheral Nerve Injury

Peripheral nerve injury is very common in clinic, which may cause paralysis in the muscles innervated by the nerve. Injury of the radial nerve and the common peroneal nerve are already discussed in the aforementioned section.

Clinical Manifestation

1) Axillary nerve injury: When the deltoid muscle is paralysed, there is less of skin sensation, drop of the shoulder joint, and failure of raising the arm. When muscular atrophy occurs, the roundness of the shoulder disappears.

2) Musculocutaneous nerve injury: There is disappearance

of elbow-bending movement and of superficial sensibility from the elbow to the anterolateral aspect of the wrist.

3) Median nerve injury: The paralysis of m. pronator teres and pronator quadratus may lead to failure of pronation of the forearm. The paralysis of mm. flexor digitorum may lead to difficulty in flexion and extension of the fingers and wrist. The atrophy of the great thenar muscle may result in failure to put the palms together. The hand looks like a "monkey's hand"(Fig. 3). There is also disappearance of the superficial sensibility in two and half or three and half fingers on the radial side.

4) Ulnar nerve injury: The paralysis of the ulnar muscles of the wrist may cause weakness in bending the wrist. In paralysis of the adductor muscle of thumb, the thumb can not make proper adduction. The atrophy of small thenar muscle may restrain the movement of the small finger. The atrophy of the interosseous muscles may prevent the fingers from drawing closer and cause serious stiffness of the metacarpophalangeal articulations. Owing to the atrophy of the third and fourth lumbrical

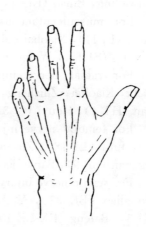

Fig. 3. "Monkey's Hand"in median nerve injury

Fig. 4 "Clawhand" in utnar nerve injury

muscles, the fourth and fifth interphalangeal joint become bent, showing a typical "clawhand"(Fig. 4). There is also disappearance of the superficial sensibility in one and half finger on the ulnar side and the corresponding parts on the palm or the back of the hand.

5) Femoral nerve injury: The knee joint fails to extend with disappearance of the superficial sensibility on the anterolateral surface of the leg.

6) Sciatic nerve injury: The knee joint loses its function of flexion. There is muscular paralysis below the leg and disappearance of the superficial sensibility on the posterolateral aspect of the leg and the foot.

7) Tibial nerve injury: The toes can not bend and the foot loses its inversion or adduction function.

Acupuncture Treatment

1) Filiform needle needling

a. Point selection

For axillary nerve injury: Huatuojiaji (EX-B 2) C_5-C_6, Jianjing (GB 21), Jianyu (LI 15), Jianzhen (SI 9), Jianneiling, Jianwailing, Binao (LI 14)

For musculocutaneous nerve injury: Huatuojiaji C_5-C_6, Quchi (LI 11), Xiaohai (SI 8), Shaohai (HT 3), Chize (LU 5), Tianjing (SJ 10), Waiguan (SJ 5), Zhizheng (SI 7)

For radial nerve injury: Huatuojiaji C_7-T_1, Jianzhen, Quchi, Xiaohai, Zhizheng, Zhigou (SJ 6), Yemen (SJ 2), Jiquan (HT 1), Houxi (SI 3)

For femoral nerve injury: Huatuojiaji L_2-L_4, Biguan (ST 31), futu (LI 18), Zusanli (ST 36), Xuehai (SP 10), Yinlingquan (SP 9), Sanyinjiao (SP 6).

For sciatic nerve injury: Huatuojiaji L_4-L_5. Ciliao (BL 32), Zhongliao (BL 33), Yinlingquan, Sanyinjiao, Zusanli, Taixi (KI 3), Bafeng (EX-LE 10).

For tibial nerve injury: Huatuojiaji L_4-L_5, Zusanli, Yanglingquan, Xuanzhong (GB 39), Jiexi (ST 41), Qiuxu (GB 40),

Bafeng.

b. Manipulation

The Huatuojiaji points can be taken either from one side or both sides. For the cervical Huatuojiaji points, perpendicular insertion is performed to 1—1. 5 cun, and for the lumbar ones, perpendicular insertion is also performed to 2—3 cun. Usually the uniform reinforcing or reducing method is adopted by lifting-thrusting and twirling-rotating. The local sensations of heaviness, numbness, distension or electric shock mean that the qi is obtained (deqi). 3 to 4 points on the limb can be needled in each session with lifting-thrusting and twirling-rotating in large amplitude. For pain, reducing method is used and for paralysis and atrophy, reinforcing method is adopted. During needling, an electric shock sensation or the involuntary tremor should appear in the affected limb. Retain the needles for 15 to 30 minutes, meanwhile manipulate the needles several times.

c. Therapeutic course

The treatment is given once or twice a day. 10 treatments constitute one therapeutic course. The spacing between two courses is 7 to 10 days.

2) Electric therapy

a. Point selection

Same as the Filiform needle needling.

b. Manipulation

After deqi, connect the needles to a G-6805 stimulator for 20 to 30 minutes with ever-increasing frequency which should be tolerable to the patient. Usually the continuous wave or dens-sparse wave is used. In each treatment, 2 to 4 points are needled.

c. Therapeutic course

The treatment is given every other day. 10 treatments constitute one therapeutic course.

3) Scalp acupuncture

a. Point selection

For the peripheral nerve injury of the upper limb: Dingzhongxian, Middle 2/5 of Dingnie Qianxiexian (healthy side), Dingpangxian II, Middle 2/5 of Dingnie Houxiexian (healthy side).

For the peripheral nerve injury of the lower limb: Dingzhongxian, Upper 1/5 of Dingnie Qianxiexian (healthy side), Dingpangxian I, Middle 2/5 of Dingnie Houxiexian (healthy side).

b. Manipulation

Use "qi withdrawal". When the needle enters the lower part of the aponeurosis, level the needle body and push it slowly forward for 1 cun. Swift lifting should be made with sudden force. Meanwhile movement of the affected limb is encouraged. Retain the needle for 2 to 24 hours.

c. Therapeutic course

The treatment is given every other day. 10 treatments constitute one therapeutic course.

d. Exercises

During needling and retaining of needles, the active or passive exercises of the affected limb should be practiced. For example, raising, anterior and posterior movements of the shoulder joint should be encouraged for axillary nerve injury; flexion and extension of the elbow for musculocutaneous nerve injury; pronation of the forearm and flexion of the wrist and fingers for median nerve injury; flexion of the wrist and fingers for radial nerve injury; flexion and extension of the knee and kicking movement for femoral nerve injury and sciatic nerve injury; flexion of the toes, adduction and inversion movements of the foot for tibial nerve injury and so on. During needling in Dingnie Houxiexian, massage or rubbing on the affected areas should be performed.

4) Point injection

a. Point selection

Select the corresponding points in reference to those used for Filiform needle needling. In each treatment, 2 points are taken.

b. Manipulation

2 ml. of the mixture (Vit. B_1 100 mg, Vit. B_{12} 0.1 mg and 1—3 mg Galanthamine) or 2 ml. of Red Sage Root injection can be used to each point in each treatment. After deqi by needling, if no bleeding is found, the drug can be injected.

c. Therapeutic course

The treatment is given everyday. 10 treatments constitute one therapeutic course.

5) Skin needling

a. Point selection

The Jing (Well) point on the affected limb, the sensitive spot on Dingnie qianxiexian and Dingnie Houxiexian (the healthy side).

b. Manipulation

First tap the Jing point with a plum blossom needle (12 times in each treatment) until there is a sensation of pain locally. Then tap the sensitive spots on the scalp which can reflect the limb disease until there appear such needling sensation on the affected limb as numbness, hotness and perspiration.

c. Therapeutic course

The treatment is given everyday. 6 treatments constitute one therapeutic course.

Therapeutic Effect

1) Acupuncture can help improve the muscular atrophy and sensory functional disturbance caused by peripheral nerve injury, and lessen the occurrence of the sequelae. However, an early treatment is essential for satisfactory therapeutic effect.

2) Dr. Yang Yuquan had treated 44 cases of peripheral nerve injury mainly with electric therapy. As a result, 20 cases were cured, 4 cases markedly improved, 6 cases improved and 14 cases without effect. The therapeutic results differ with different nerve injury. Generally it is best for radial nerve injury and then the facial nerve, recurrent nerve, accessory nerve, peroneal nerve, brachial plexus, median nerve by sequence. (Journal of Shanghai Acupuncture, 1983; 2)

3) Dr. Chen Tiwei mainly applied skin needling to treat 50 cases of paralysis. As a result, 30 cases were cured. 15 cases were with excellent effect. 3 cases were improved and 2 cases were with no effect. The total effective rate was 96%. (Journal of Yunnan TCM, 1991; 1 : 12). This method can also be used to treat the paralysis caused by peripheral nerve injury.

4) Dr. Zeng Shaojie had treated 36 cases of common peroneal nerve injury and 3 cases tibial nerve injury with electric needle therapy and point injection. As a result, 33 cases were cured, and 6 cases were improved with a total effective rate of 100%. (Journal of Chinese Acupuncture, 1987; 4)

5) The authors also obtained very satisfactory therapeutic results in the treatment of peripheral nerve injury with scalp acupuncture and electric therapy. And we pointed out that if there is sensory disturbance and muscular atrophy, point injection and moxibustion should be added.

Discussion

Acupuncture may produce better therapeutic results for closed injuries of the peripheral nerves. However, it has no effect for the nerve severed completely.

SECTION VI
Infantile Cerebral Palsy

Infantile cerebral palsy is a collective term referring to a condition, a non-progressive central motor function disturbance caused by various factors before born or in the perinatal period. In serious cases, it often accompanied by hypophrenia, convulsion, dysacousis, dystopia ... etc. Children with this disease have obviously lowered physical development than the normal children. In addition, they often have difficulties in their studies.

Epidemic encephalitis B is a common acute and seasonal infectious disease. It is an acute diffuse inflammation in the brain parenchyma. After such acute stage of fever, coma, and convulsion, some complications such as paralysis of limbs, aphasia and amentia may remain in some cases.

Acupuncture has been proved to have certain effect on the above-mentioned conditions.

1. Infantile Cerebral Palsy

The main causes for infantile cerebral palsy include:

1) Cerebral ischemia: This may be caused by threatened abortion, placenta previa, premature separation of placenta and prolapse of umbilical cord.

2) Intracranial hemorrhage: It is often resulted from dystocia, birth trauma, cerebrovascular diseases and general blood disease.

3) Infection: The mother in early pregnancy suffers from urticaria, herpes zoster, influenza ... etc. and these diseases may influence brain development of the fetus. After birth the infection in the central nervous system can also cause this disease.

4) Premature birth

5) Nuclear jaundice: Hyperbilirubinemia of new born may be caused by maternal-fetal blood group incompatibility and other factors. The blood bilirubin exceeds 20 mg/dl.

6) Others: this include intracranial abnormally, congenital hydrocephalus, severe malnutrition of the mother in the early pregnancy and X-ray irradiation.

In infantile cerebral palsy, there will be paralysis in all the four limbs, or in the limbs of one side, or in both lower limbs or in a single limb or in three limbs.

Clinical Manifestation

1) Pay attention to find out the cause of the infantile cerebral palsy, such as the disease history of the mother in pregnancy and in the perinatal period, birth history, and infections of the baby.

2) In the early stage, there is increased grasp reflex. The

tonic neck reflexes may remain for six months after birth.

3) There is increased muscular tension of the paralysed muscle, especially in the adductor muscle, showing a spastic paralysis.

4) When the diseased baby is raised vertically, both of his lower limbs stretch out with adduction or inversion or in most cases, with scissors-like crossing. For mild cases, there is only light paralysis with unsteady gait.

5) The symptoms in the upper limbs are not so severe as in the lower limbs. There is flexion of both elbows with the hands in front of the chest. Sometimes there is flexion of the wrist and finger joints. For mild cases, there is only slight trouble in the movement of the hands.

6) There may be various kind of hyperactivity of deep reflex and ankle-clonus. The baby still has a positive Babinski's Sign even after the age of two years old.

7) The nuclear jaundice often results in extrapyramidal sequelae. In children patients, involuntary choreic movements are often noticed.

8) In some cases, there will be hypomyotonia or hyperactivity of the knee jerk reflex.

9) The onset may be a combined type of spasm, extrapyramidal system and hypomyotonia. However the mixture of the first two types is the most common.

Acupuncture Treatment

1) Filiform needle needling

Prescription 1
a. Point selection
Main points: Yamen (DU 15), Tianzhu (BL 10), Dazhui (DU 14), Dazhu (BL 11); Yanglingquan (GB 34), Xuanzhong (GB 39), Taichong (LR 3)

Adjunct points: Add Dazhong (KI 4), and Shenmen (HT 7) for those with poor memory, or with such behavior as talking to oneself and sluggish eyes. Add Jinjin (EX-HN 12), Yuye (EX-HN 13), Tiantu (RN 22) and Tongli (HT 5) for those with dysphonia and add Gongsun (SP 4) for those with poor appetite.

b. Manipulation

The main points must be needled in each treatment. In needling Yamen, advance the needle with twirling in a direction to the midpoint of a line joining the two eyes to a depth of 1 to 1.3 cun. Then twirl and rotate the needle slowly until deqi (there is a warmness-heat sensation locally). Try to make the needling sensation transmit downwards to the whole body and the four limbs. It would be better if there is feverish or even perspiration in the palms or the underside of the foot. When Tianzhu is needled, perpendicular insertion should be performed to 0.5—0.6 cun (For fat patients, the insertion depth should not be more than 1 cun). After deqi, make the needle sensation transmit along the same-side neck, back, waist, lower limb and outer side of the foot ipsilaterally. For Dazhui, insert the needle perpendicularly to 0.6—0.7 cun. After deqi, there is a warmness feeling all over the body. Dazhu can be needled perpendicularly to 0.5—0.6 cun. After deqi, the tiredness on the upper part of the body can be eliminated immediately. Yanglingquan is needled perpendicularly for 1 cun. After deqi, the tiredness in the lower part of the body can also be eliminated. It is required that there should be a clearer mind after Taichong and Xuanzhong are needled. After Taichong is needled, there should be a brighter eyesight.

Among the adjunct points, Dazhong and Shenmen must be needled gently. In the main points, retain the needles for 20 to 30 minutes, and in adjunct points, needle retaining is not necessary.

c. Therapeutic course

The treatment is given 2 to 3 times a week. 20 treatments constitute one therapeutic course. Generally it is not necessary to arrange a rest between two courses.

Prescription 2

a. Point selection

For paralysis of the upper limb: Jianyu (LI 15), Quchi (LI 11), Waiguan (SJ 5), Hegu (LI 4)

For paralysis of the lower limbs: Huantiao (GB 30), Biguan (ST 31), Futu (LI 18), Zusanli (ST 36)

For flaccid Paralysis of the waist: Shenshu (BL 23), Yaoyangguan (DU 3)

For contracture of the elbow joints: Shousanli (LI 10), Zhizheng (SI 7)

For difficulty in flexion and extension of the finger joints: from Hegu to Houxi (SI 3)

For wrist drop: Waiguan, Yangchi (SJ 4), Yangxi (LI 5)

For talipes varus: Juegu (LI 16), or Kunlun (BL 60) or 1 cun of the lateral aspect of Chengshan (BL 57)

For talipes valgus: Sanyinjiao (SP 6), Taixi (KI 3) or Zhaohai (KI 6), 1 cun of the medial aspect of Chengshan

For foot drop: Jiexi (ST 41), Shangqiu (SP 5), Qiuxu (GB 40)

For scissors gait: fengshi (GB 31), Yanglingquan (GB 34), Xuanzhong (GB 39)

For hypophrenia: Baihui (DU 20), Fengchi (GB 20), Sishencong (EX-HN 1)

For aphasia: Tongli (HT 5), Lianquan (RN 23), Jinjin (EX-HN 12), Yuye (EX-HN 13)

For flaccid paralysis of the neck: Tianzhu (BL 10), Dazhui (DU 14) or Shenzhu (DU 12)

b. Manipulation

Mainly a reinforcing method is adopted with lifting-thrusting and twirling-rotating. No needle retention.

c. Therapeutic course

The treatment is given once everyday. Three months constitute a therapeutic course.

Prescription 3

a. Point selection

Take a point 3 cun directly below Fengchi (GB 20), on the same level of the 5th cervical vertebra. First insert a needle perpendicularly for 1. 5 to 2 cun, then insert another needle obliquely for 1. 5 to 2 cun to the direction of the vertebra. (The angle between the needle body and the skin is 45°.) Again then, insert a third needle transversely along the skin to the vertebra for 2 cun. This is known as "three needles in one point". The points on both sides of the body can be needled in turn.

b. Manipulation

After deqi, try to induce a warmth sensation in the neck, shoulder and elbow by twirling and rotating the needle in large amplitude. 1 to 2 adjunct points can also be selected based on the clinical symptoms. These points can be needled with the method of uniform reinforcing and reducing.

c. Therapeutic course

One treatment is given everyday. 7 treatments constitute one therapeutic course. The spacing between two courses is 3 to 4 days.

2) Scalp acupuncture

Prescription 1

a. Point selection

For paralysis of the lower limb: Upper 1/5 of Dingnie Qianxiexian on the contralateral side, Dingpangxian I

For paralysis of the upper limb: Middle 2/5 of Dingnie Qianxiexian on the contralateral side, Dingpangxian II

For salivation, deviation of the tongue and anandia: Lower 2/5 of Dingnie Qianxiexian on the contralateral side

For diseases in the cerebellum: Zhenxiapangxian

For psychosis: Ezhongxian, Epangxian I (right)

b. Manipulation

Insert a No. 28 filiform needle along the skin into the galea aponeurotica for 1 to 1. 5 cun. Try to get deqi with the method of "qi withdrawal". Retain the needle for 30 to 40 minutes, during which the needle can be manipulated for 2 to 3 times. Each manipulation lasts 5 to 8 minutes.

c. Therapeutic course

One treatment is given everyday. 15 treatments constitute one therapeutic course. The spacing between two courses is 3 to 5 days.

d. Exercises

In the time of needling and retaining of needle, exercises of the affected limb should be carried on.

Prescription 2

a. Point selection

Except the above-mentioned scalp needling lines, 3 insertions on the temporal area (corresponding to the posterior part of the superior temporal gyrus, middle temporal gyrus and inferior temporal gyrus) and 5 insertions on the forehead (corresponding to the anterior part of the superior frontal gyrus, middle frontal gyrus, and inferior frontal gyrus), and the anterior motor area of cerebrum are selected.

b. Manipulation

For the 3 insertions on the temporal area: The first needle is inserted from 1 cm on the anterior part of the lower margin of the parietal bone eminence to the backward direction for 1 cun. The second needle is inserted from 1.5 cm above the ear tip to the backward direction for 1 cun. The third needle is inserted from a spot 2 cm on the posterior part of another spot which is 2 cm below the ear tip to the backward direction for 1 cun.

For the 5 insertions on the forehead: Insert 5 needles from a spot 2 cm away from the hairline. Each of 5 needles should be inserted from the anterior to the posterior in sequence for 1 cun in the area topographically between the left and right lateral fissures of cerebrum.

For the insertions in the anterior motor area of the cerebrum: Altogether 3 needles are inserted. The needle in the middle should be inserted from 4 cm on the anterior part of the midpoint of Dingnie qianxiexian, to the backward direction for 1 cun. The other two needles are inserted rom 1.5 cm away on both sides.

For the needling, No. 28 filiform needles of 1.5 cun long are often selected. The needle should be inserted rapidly into the galea aponeurotica, and retained for 2 hours without manipulation and avoid strong stimulation.

c. Therapeutic course

The treatment is given once every other day. 10 treatments constitute one therapeutic course. Usually the spacing between two courses is 1 week.

d. Exercises

During needle retaining, the sick child is permitted to play freely so as to raise the therapeutic effect.

3) Ear acupuncture

Prescription 1

a. Point selection

Sympathetic, Shenmen, Brain Stem, Subcortex, Heart, Liver, Kidney, Adrenal Gland, Small Intestine, Stomach

The upper part, middle part and lower part of the back of ear.

Other points can also be selected according to the site of paralysis.

b. Manipulation

In each treatment, the points on one ear are selected. Both ears can be needled alternatively. A seed of vaccaria segetalis is taped tightly to each point. Everyday, patient should press the points for 2 to 3 times so as to stimulate the points.

c. Therapeutic course

Change the seeds every 2 to 3 days. 15 treatments constitute one therapeutic course.

Prescription 2

a. Point selection

Main point: Brain Stem

Adjunct points: Subcortex, Kidney

Add Liver for those with motor disturbance; add Heart for those with hypophrenia.

Points on both ears are needled alternatively.

b. Manipulation

All of the above auricular points are needled with a 0.5 cun filiform needle. The insertion depth is about 0.1 to 0.2 cun. After deqi by twirling and rotating, retain the needle for 30 minutes.

c. Therapeutic course

One treatment is given everyday. 20 treatments constitute one therapeutic course.

4) Skin needling

a. Point selection

The line alongside the Du Meridian between Changqiang (DU 1) and Dazhui (DU 14),

The line alongside the Ren Meridian between Qugu (RN 2) and Tiantu (RN 22).

The line alongside the Foot-Yangming Meridian between Biguan (ST 31) and Neiting (ST 44).

b. Manipulation

Tap along the meridians with a skin needle until the local skin becomes reddish without bleeding. Moderate stimulation should be applied. Each meridian should be tapped 3 to 5 times in each treatment.

c. Therapeutic course

One treatment is given every other day. 10 treatments constitute one therapeutic course.

5) Point injection

Prescription 1

a. Point selection

(a) Yamen (DU 15), Shenshu (BL 23); (b) Fengchi (GB

20), Zusanli (ST 36); (c) Dazhui (DU 14), Neiguan (PC 6)

The Du points are selected mainly for cerebropathy. For example. those with simple hypophrenia should be treated by needling the point groups in turn. Meanwhile 2 to 3 adjunct points can also be selected according to the symptoms.

b. Manipulation

For the three points --- Yamen, Fengchi, and Dazhui, the insertion should be no deeper than 1 to 1. 5 cun and 1 to 2 ml. of drug is injected in each point.

Acetyl-glutamine for points in the head and Fursultiamine hydrochloride for points on the trunk and four limbs.

c. Therapeutic course

One treatment is given every other day. 10 treatments constitute one therapeutic course. The spacing between two courses is 7 to 10 days.

Prescription 2

a. Point selection

For hemiplegia, the spots which divide the Dingnie Qianxiexian into upper, middle and lower equal parts are selected. For hypophrenia, Dingzhongxian and Ezhongxian are taken. For cerebral urinary incontinence, Baihui (DU 20) is selected.

b. Manipulation

Several points should be needled in turn. 1 ml. of drug (1 ampule consists of 100 μg of Acetyl-glutamine, or 20 μg of Fursultiamine, or 250 μg of γ-aminobutyric acid) is injected into each point. For those with urinary incontinence, 2 to 3 ml. (the mixture of the above three drugs) can be used.

c. Therapeutic course

One treatment is given every other day. 10 treatments constitute one therapeutic course. The spacing between two courses is 7 to 10 days.

Therapeutic Effect

1) Acupuncture can be used to treat infantile cerebral palsy

with satisfactory results. There are many therapeutic methods such as filiform needle needling, scalp acupuncture, point injection. Some doctors prefer to the combined use of Filiform needle needling and Point injection, or Scalp acupuncture and Point injection ... and claimed that the combined therapy is more effective than single method.

2) Dr. Du Guanwen had treated 55 cases of hypophrenia due to this disease. As a result, 39 cases were cured and 16 cases were improved. (Journal of Chinese Acupuncture, 1989; 4:9)

Dr. Li Sixian had treated 50 cases of infantile cerebral dysgenesis with head-point injection. The results showed that 37 cases obtained very good effect; 7 cases were improved and 6 cases were with no effect. (Journal of Chinese Acupuncture, 1983; 2:3)

It was reported that there were some doctors who used the above-mentioned method for the treatment of congenital hypophrenia with rather good results. Therefore, acupuncture can not only restore the motor function of the paralysed children, but also improve their intelligence development.

3) Scalp acupuncture is effective for this disease. Dr. Shen Xiulan reported 144 cases with satisfactory results. (44 cases were cured, 62 cases with excellent effect, 37 cases with improvement and 1 case with no effect). (Journal of Henan TCM, 1987; 4)

Again, Dr. Lin Xuejian reported 73 cases with 34 cases cured, 38 cases improved and 1 case failed. (Journal of Shanghai TCM, 1981; 10)

Some people consider that the selection of points in the Scalp acupuncture is dependent not only on the functions of the cerebral cortex, but also the theory of neurophysiology, the examples are the selection of "5 insertions on the forehead"and "insertions on the anterior motor area of the cerebrum".

4) Nowadays, reports on the treatment of infantile cerebral palsy with Point injection are not too few. Dr. Shi Bingpei reported 270 cases with 30 cases excellently improved, 145 cases

improved and 95 failed. (Journal of Liaoning TCM, 1984; 5:8)

Dr. Lin Liyu had treated 50 cases due to hypoxia with 2 cases cured, 16 cases markedly improved, 30 cases improved and 2 cases failed. (Journal of Shanghai Acupuncture, 1987; 1)

Discussion

1) The infantile cerebral palsy is a challenging disease in its management. With its complex pathogenic causes and harmful consequence, it often affects the functions of the children who suffer from this disease, such as sitting, standing, walking and speaking. Sometimes it is also complicated by hypophrenia, deviation of neck, epilepsy, salivation and so on and so forth. Because the pathology is in the brain, it is very difficult to achieve complete cure. However, an early diagnosis and timely treatment can lessen the functional disturbance, and the prognosis is especially favorable for patients with slight paralysis.

2) The degree of the cerebral injury and the age of the patient plays an important role in the prognosis of the illness. Generally, the more serious is the injury and the older is the patient, the poorer the prognosis.

3) During treatment, better cares should be provided to the sick children. Sufficient nutrition, rational education and proper functional exercises will help to raise the needling effect. In addition, the daily movement training and language training to the sick children should also be strengthened. The physiotherapy should be undertaken to prevent muscular atrophy.

4) If it is complicated with epilepsy or joint deformity, corresponding treatment should be given.

2. Epidemic B Encephalitis

The encephalitis B is an acute infectious disease caused by encephalitis B virus which is transmitted by the mosquitoes. With its seasonal nature, this disease has a very high incidence in areas with plenty of mosquitoes. The disease is mostly common in children. The onset of disease is sudden. There are such symptoms as high fever, coma, convulsion ... It belongs to the category of "Summer Fever"in TCM. After the acute stage, if there are dullness of mind, aphasia, paralysis ... etc. which can not be cured for a long time, the disease, in most cases, is caused by "impairment of yin due to excessive heat", "invasion of the pathogenic wind due to yin deficiency"and "obstruction of the meridians".

Clinical Manifestation

1) The disease occurs with a typical seasonal nature, i. e. in July to September.

2) It is most common in children below 10 years old (60—70%).

3) The onset of disease is often sudden with high fever, coma, convulsion ... etc. It is often accompanied with signs of meningeal irritation.

4) In typical cases, the disease can be divided into 4 stages:

a. The stage with primary fever which occurs about 3 days after the onset. The temperature is about 38—39℃ with headache and general malaise. Some patients show slight lethargy, nausea, vomiting or mild rigidity of the neck.

b. The summit phase is from the fourth day to the 10th day. The temperature gets higher even above 40℃ in some patients. The symptoms aggravated gradually, and the unconsciousness, lethargy, even convulsion, stiffness, ... etc. may occur. There is also signs of meningeal irritation, or disappearance of the abdominal reflex. cremasteric reflex and tendon reflex. In infants, there will be bulging of anterior fontanel. In severe cases, there will be central respiratory failure.

c. The convalescent stage: The temperature return normal and the symptoms alleviate gradually, however, in severe cases there are dullness of mind, dementia, aphasia, dysphagia, paralysis of the facial muscles, and rigid paralysis of the four limbs (flaccid paralysis in some cases). With energetic treatment for about half a year, this disease can be cured.

d. The stage with sequelae: This stage refers to the presence of psychoneurological symptoms half a year after the onset, most of which are aphasia, paralysis and amentia.

5) According to the severity of the disease, and the symptoms in the nervous system, the encephalitis B is usually divided into 4 types — mild type (Wei-qi type), common or moderate type, serious type (Qi-ying type) and critical type (Ying-xue type). For the mild or moderate types, the body temperature is about 38—40℃ without any symptoms in convalescent stage. The disease course is often 7 to 10 days. In severe type, there are coma, convulsion … etc. The temperature is over 40℃, and there is obvious pathological reflex or respiratory failure. The disease course is over two weeks with some symptoms in the convalescent stage or even sequelae. For the critical type, there are typical sudden onset, high fever, quickly-developed deep coma, severe convulsion … etc. Patients may die soon due to failure of the central nervous system.

6) Clinically cases of mild or moderate type are encountered more frequently. Some severe cases can be found in the early stage of the epidemic. The critical type is very rare.

7) The lab findings show that the WBC count may increase to 10000 to 30000, with predominant polymorphonuclear neutrophil leukocytes. The cerebrospinal fluid examination reveals increased intracranial pressure, moderate increase of WBC count (about 500, most of which are neutrophils), slight increase of protein and normal glycogen and chloride. Complement fixation test often become positive between the 2nd to 5th week of the disease.

Acupuncture Treatment

Acupuncture treatment is undertaken in the convalescent stage and for the sequelae. Following is a brief introduction on the treatment of the cerebral palsy caused by infantile encephalitis B. This can also be applied in the treatment for adult patients.

1) Filiform needle needling

Prescription 1

a. Point selection

Main points: Fengchi (GB 20), Fengfu (DU 16), Baihui (DU 20), Dazhui (DU 14)

Adjunct points: Add Jiache (ST 6), Yifeng (SJ 17), Xiaguan (ST 7), Dicang (ST 4) and Yingxiang (LI 20) for facial paralysis; add Dicang, Jiache and Chengjiang (RN 24) for salivation; add Lianquan (RN 23) and Tiantu (RN 22) for dysphagia; add Baliao, Shenzhu (BL 23), Taodao (DU 13) and Huatuojiaji for soft neck; add Shenmen (HT 7) and Daling (PC 70) for mental retardation; add Jingming (BL 1), Sizhukong (SJ 23), Chengqi (ST 1), and Hegu (LI 4) for oculomotor paralysis; add Jingming, Yangbai (GB 14) and Zanzhu (BL 2) for blindness; add Tinggong (SI 19), Tinghui (GB 2), Ermen (SJ 21), Yamen (DU 15) and Waiguan (SJ 5) for deafness and dumbness; add Jiexi (ST 41), Yanglingquan (GB 34), Juegu (GB 39), Taixi (KI 3), Fengshi (GB 31) and Huantiao (GB 30) for weakness of the foot.

b. Manipulation

The method of uniform reinforcing and reducing is performed without retaining of needle. The main points must be needled in each treatment. Moxibustion on Baihui should be performed for those with mental retardation. Tapping with skin needle on the forehead is added for oculomotor nerve paralysis. Massage or electric therapy may be added.

c. Therapeutic course

The treatment is given once every other day. 10 treatments constitute one therapeutic course. The spacing between two courses is 3 to 5 days.

Prescription 2

a. Point selection

Main points: Shenmen (HT 7), Zhizheng (SI 7), Taichong

(LR 3), Guangming (GB 37), Taibai (SP 3), Fenglong (ST 40), Taiyuan (LU 9), Pianli (LI 6), Taixi (KI 3), Feiyang (BL 58), Daling (PC 70), Waiguan (SJ 5)

Adjunct points: (a) Baihui (DU 20), Renzhong (DU 26), Shangxing (DU 23), Touwei (ST 8), Tongziliao (GB 1), Yangbai (GB 14), Zanzhu (BL 2), Yuyao (EX-HN 4), Jingming (BL 1), Xiaguan (ST 7), Jiache (ST 6), Lianquan (RN 23), Ermen (SJ 21), Tinghui (GB 2), Yifeng (SJ 17), Jianyu (LI 15), Binao (LI 14), Quchi (LI 11), Shousanli (LI 10), Hegu (LI 4), Neiguan (PC 6), Laogong (PC 8), Zhongwan (RN 12), Guanyuan (RN 4), Huantiao (GB 30), Fengshi (GB 31), Zusanli (ST 36), Yinlingquan (SP 9), Yanglingquan (GB 34), Juegu (GB 39), Sanyinjiao (SP 6), Zhaohai (KI 6), Zulingqi (GB 41), Yongquan (KI 1). (b) Fengchi (GB 20), Fengfu (DU 16), Yamen (DU 15), Tianzhu (BL 10), Dazhui (DU 14), Zhiyang (DU 9), Jinsuo (DU 8), Mingmen (DU 4), Yaoyangguan (DU 3), Xinshu (BL 15), Geshu (BL 17), Ganshu (BL 18), Pishu (BL 20), Weishu (BL 21), Shenshu (BL 23), Chengfu (BL 36), Yinmen (BL 37), Weizhong (BL 40), Chengshan (BL 57), Houxi (SI 3), Kunlun (BL 60), Shenmai (BL 62)

b. Manipulation

The main points on both sides must be needled in each treatment and the adjunct points can be selected in turn on symptoms differentiation, such as disturbance of consciousness, pathologic blindness, dumbness, deafness and the motor disturbance of the four limbs. Usually uniform reinforcing and reducing method is adopted and rapid twirling and rotating 6—7 times is performed before the needle is withdrawn.

c. Therapeutic course

The treatment is given once every other day. 10 treatments constitute one therapeutic course. The spacing between two courses is 3 to 5 days.

2) Scalp acupuncture

a. Point selection

For paralysis: Dingzhongxian, Dingnie Qianxiexian, Ding-pangxian I and Dingpangxian II

For aphasia: Dingzhongxian, Ezhongxian, Epangxian I (right), Nieqianxian and Lower 2/5 of Dingnie Qianxiexian

For dysphagia: Ezhongxian

For dullness of mind: Dingzhongxian, Ezhongxian, Epangxian I (right)

For deafness: Niehouxian

For blindness: Zhenshang Zhengzhongxian, Zhenshang Pangxian

b. Manipulation

For infants and young children, shallow needling is adopted and the needle is inserted very superficially on several spots of the scalp lines. For children who is a little older, the method of "qi withdrawal" can be used with no retaining of needle.

c. Therapeutic course

The treatment is given once every other day. 10 treatments constitute one therapeutic course.

3) Ear needling

a. Point selection

Heart, Kidney, Occiputs, Shenmen, Brain Stem, Subcortex, points corresponding to the pathology location.

b. Manipulation

After being inserted, the needle should be twirled and rotated for three minutes.

c. Therapeutic course

The treatment is given once everyday. 10 to 15 treatments constitute one therapeutic course. This therapy can be integrated with other acupuncture methods.

4) Point injection

a. Point selection

Yamen (DU 15), Shenshu (BL 23); Fengchi (GB 20), Zusanli (ST 36); Dazhui (DU 14), Neiguan (PC 6)

b. Manipulation

The above 3 groups of points can be needled alternatively.

For points on the head, 2 ml. of drugs (Acetyl-glutamine, 50 µg/ml) can be injected (both sides). For those points on the trunk and the limbs, 1 ml. of the drug (Fursultiamine hydrochloride: 25µg/ml) is injected.

c. Therapeutic course

The treatment is given once everyday. 10 to 15 treatments constitute one therapeutic course. The spacing between two courses is 7 to 10 days.

5) Moxibustion

a. Point selection

Baihui (DU 20), Dazhui (DU 14), Guanyuan (RN 4), Shenshu (BL 23)

b. Manipulation

1 to 2 moxa stick of 30 cm long is used in each treatment. The four points mentioned above are used in turn.

c. Therapeutic course

The treatment is given once everyday. 10 treatments constitute one therapeutic course.

6) Point irradiation

a. Point selection

Baihui (DU 20), Fengchi (GB 20), Dazhui (DU 14), Neiguan (PC 6), Sanyinjiao (SP 6); Hegu (LI 4), Quchi (LI 11), Waiguan (SJ 5), Zusanli (ST 36), Xuanzhong (GB 39)

b. Manipulation

The two groups of points should be needled in turn with the method of uniform reinforcing and reducing. The needle is retained for 10 to 15 minutes during which the points are irradiated with the ultra-red rays. The irradiation distance is adjusted to make the patient feels comfortable and the skin appears an erythemoid halo.

c. Therapeutic course

The treatment is given once everyday. 10 to 15 treatments constitute one therapeutic course.

7) Skin needling

a. Point selection

Tapping areas: cervical vertebrae, lumbosacral region, submaxillary region, both sides of the trachea, around the mouth

Yamen (DU 15), Fengfu (DU 16), Hegu (LI 4), Shaoshang (LU 11), Yifeng (SJ 17), Jiache (ST 6)

b. Manipulation

Light stimulation to make the local skin reddish.

Therapeutic Effect

1) Acupuncture is mainly used to treat the sequelae of the encephalitis B, and is effective to cerebral palsy and other accompanying symptoms. Better therapeutic results may be obtained for those with shorter duration of disease and are treated timely.

2) Dr. Gao Qiru had treated 148 cases of sequelae of encephalitis B by mainly needling Fengchi, Baihui, Dazhui and other points. As a result, 111 cases (75%) were cured, 6 cases obtained excellent result, 29 cases improved and 2 cases failed. The over-all effective rate was 98.65%. (Journal of Chinese Acupuncture, 1984; 3)

Dr. Wang Naiyi reported an all-cure experience in 15 cases of the sequelae of encephalitis B after 20 to 25 needling treatments. (Journal of Chinese Acupuncture, 1989; 3:9)

Dr. Su Erliang had treated 112 cases of encephalitis B in convalescent stage with a total effective rate of 89.2%. The points he selected were Shenshu, Sanyinjiao, Pishu, Zhongwan, Qihai, Xuanzhong and Shenmen. (Journal of Jiangsu TCM, 1986; 10)

3) Generally better therapeutic results can be achieved when a combined needling method is adopted in the treatment of the sequelae of encephalitis B. For example. Dr. Yang Jinan used penetration needling combined with other points and achieved a rather satisfactory result. The penetration needling he used is from Qianding (DU 21) to Baihui (DU 20), from Houding (DU 19) to Baihui and from Louque (BL 8) of both sides to Baihui. (Journal of TCM, 1983;2)

SECTION VII
Hysterical Paralysis

Hysteria is a disease caused mainly by the psychogenic or other mental factors. It is characterized by various psychosomatic symptoms. Hysterical paralysis is one of them. This disease belongs to "Viscera impetuosity syndrome", "Lily disease", "syncope"or "melancholia"in traditional Chinese medicine.

Clinical Manifestation

1) Most of the patients are young or mid-aged females.

2) The disease occurs with a sudden onset of monoplegia or paraplegia.

3) During the attack, most of the patients are not able to stand or walk, but can move their limbs freely in a lying position, and some can walk in a strange gait.

4) The tendon reflex of the limbs may be normal or may be increased. The muscular tension is often normal. Or there may be tremor, irregular spasm and choreic movements in the truncal part of the limbs.

5) There may be sensory disturbance such as numbness and anesthesia of limbs.

6) There is often weak psychomotility and strong suggest - ibility.

Acupuncture Treatment

1) Filiform needle needling

Prescription 1
a. Point selection
Main point: Yongquan (KI 1)
Adjunct points: Add Waiguan (SJ 5), and Quchi (LI 11) for the disorder in the upper limbs and Zusanli (ST 36) and Xuanzhong (GB 39) for the lower limbs.

b. Manipulation

First try to make the patient restore the sensory sensation in the affected part by needling Yongquan with a No. 18 to 22 filiform needle. If the therapeutic effect is not ideal, add the adjunct points. The needle is retained for 3 to 5 minutes.

c. Therapeutic course

If no improvement is obtained after the first needling treatment, give the second treatment 3 to 7 days later.

Prescription 2

a. Point selection

In the lower limb: Quanzhong, which is localized 1 cun posterior to Yongquan

In the upper limb: Cunping, which is localized 1 cun above the midpoint of the dorsal carpal cross striation, 0.4 cun to the radial side

Adjunct points: Futu (LI 18), Quchi (LI 11), Chongmen (SP 12), Yanglingquan (GB 34)

b. Manipulation

Insert a No. 22—26 filiform needle perpendicularly into Quanzhong and Cunping 2 to 3 cm in depth. Perform lifting-thrusting and twirling-rotating. After deqi, move the affected limb first passively, then actively until the limb can move freely. Withdraw the needle and ask the patient to do some exercises.

2) Scalp acupuncture

a. Point selection

Ezhongxian, Epangxian I (right), Dingzhongxian, Upper 1/5 of Dingnie Qianxiexian (lower limb), Middle 2/5 of Dingnie Qianxiexian (upper limb)

b. Manipulation

Firstly ezhongxian is needled. Ask the patient to hold breath, insert the needle swiftly into the lower part of the galea aponeurotica and perform the method of "qi withdrawal". If the patient can not hold breath for so long, let him take a deep breathing. When Epangxian I (right) is needled, same manipulation as mentioned above is applied. When Dingzhongxian is needled, ask the patient to concentrate his mind on "dantian" — the elixir field. The frequency of qi withdrawal should be lowered down. In needling Dingnie Qianxiexian (upper 1/5 for lower limb and middle 2/5 for upper limb), qi withdrawal should be performed on the points from both sides. Meanwhile ask the pattient to move the affected limb actively.

c. Exercises

Ask the patient to concentrate the mind on the affected limbs when Dingzhongxian and Dingnie Qianxiexian are needled. Let the patient imagine that his limb was moving and then encourage him to move it actively.

3) Electrotherapy

a. Point selection

Same as those in Filiform needle needling prescription 1 and prescription 2.

b. Manipulation

Make interrupted or continuous stimulation with a G-6805 stimulator (voltage: 6 v; positive pulse $\geqslant$ 25 v; negative pulse $\geqslant$ 40 v.). The strength of stimulation should be tolerable to the patient. Ask the patient to see the jerks in the affected limb which is induced by the stimulation so as to strengthen the suggestion. If there is still no improvement, the adjunct points in Filiform needle needling prescription 2 can be taken. It is required that when Futu (brachial nerve) is needled, the needle should be inserted to 2—3 cm deep and an electric-shock sensation should be experienced in the upper limb of the patient. When Quchi (radial nerve) is needled, the insertion should be about 3—4 cm deep and there should be an electric-shock sensation in the forearm. In needling chongmen (femoral nerve) of the lower limb, the insertion should be 2—3 cm deep and there should be contraction of the quadriceps muscle of thigh. And when Yanglingquan (common peroneal nerve) is needled, the insertion should be 2—3 cm deep and an electric-shock sensation should be felt on the lateral side of the leg. The frequency used is 60—100 times/minute. There should be regular contraction in the muscle groups controlled by the said nerves. It is important to let the patient see the jerks on his limbs with his own eyes.

4) Ear needling

a. Point selection

Heart, Subcortex, Occipitalis. These ear points can be supported by Liver, Endocrine, Shenmen, Uterus and the corresponding sensitive points of the ear.

b. Manipulation

In each treatment, 3 to 4 points on both ears are selected and strong stimulation should be made by bird-peck needling Retain the needle for 20 minutes. Or electric needling can be applied.

5) Point injection

a. Point selection

Neiguan (PC 6), Zusanli (ST 36), Quchi (LI 11), Hegu (LI 4), Yanglingquan (GB 34)

b. Manipulation

Take 2 points in each treatment and inject 0.5 ml. of Vit. B_1 to each point.

6) Skin needling

a. Point selection

During the attack: back of the neck, sacral region, Fengchi (GB 20), Neiguan (PC 6), Renzhong (DU 26) and the finger tips

At the time without attack: back of the neck, sacral region, the head, Dazhui (DU 14), Zhongwan (RN 12), Ganshu (BL 18), Danshu (BL 19), Neiguan (PC 6) and the medial side of the leg.

b. Manipulation

Give moderate stimulation until the local skin becomes reddish or shows petechiae.

Therapeutic Effect

1)It is very effective for the treatment of this disease. We often cured it by just needling the Yongquan once. (Please refer to typical cases in Chapter six). Dr. Zhang Zhengying had treated 1316 cases with acupuncture on point Yongquan combined with psychotherapy and functional training and achieved cure in 1287 cases (97. 85). 900 cases regained their health only after one needling treatment. A long-term follow-up on 125 cases revealed 98 cases without relapse, 4 cases with subjective symptoms such as numbness, soreness and pain in the affected limb and relapse in 23 cases. (Journal of TCM, 1986; 8)

2) In *China's Plum-blossom Needle*, a typical case report was introduced. This patient had hysteria for 5 years. He was found to have dizziness followed by unconsciousness, distress in chest, failure to speak, salivation and jerks of the four limbs 14 days before he visited the doctor. The seizure occurs 1 to 2, or even 3 to 4 times a day. However, the convulsion was stopped just by skin needling once and all of his symptoms were disappeared after ten treatments.

Discussion

1) Differential diagnosis should be made to distinguish this disease from other organic diseases of the nervous system. In the case of hysterical paralysis, there is often a sudden onset. However, when acupuncture or electrotherapy is applied together with the suggestion therapy, the paralysed limb can usually be cured.

2) The patient should be encouraged to have functional exercises actively and to adjust himself properly to his environment.

3) During the acupuncture treatment, psychotherapy as well as suggestion therapy should be carried on. The purpose of the psychotherapy is to help the patient set up confidence on the acupuncture treatment. It will be better if the acupuncture is given under the urgent demand of patient.

4) After the needling, the patient should be asked to walk for several steps with the help of others. Then he can be asked

to walk by himself.

5) Acupuncture is also effective to other hysterical symptoms.

SECTION VIII
Paralysis of The Facial Nerve

Also known as facial paralysis, it is one of the most common diseases of the cranial nerves. The central facial paralysis can be caused by cerebrovascular accident, cerebrovascular malformation and intracranial tumor. This disorder belongs to supranuclear paralysis of the facial nerves. The peripheral facial nerve paralysis can be caused by the facial neuritis inside the temporal bone (the facial canal), or by viral infection and compression of the facial nerves leading to disturbance of the blood circulation and axon myelinic degeneration. This disorder belongs to intranuclear paralysis of the facial nerves. In TCM, it is called Waipi (deviation of the eye and mouth).

Clinical Manifestation

1) Central Facial Paralysis

a. There are often pathogenic changes occurred above the level of facial nerve nucleus on the middle part of pons, such as cerebrospinal accidents or intracranial tumors.

b. This disorder is often complicated by motor disturbance of the opposite limb.

c. Symptoms of the facial paralysis appeared on the lower part of the opposite side of the face including deviation of the mouth corner and shallow nasolabial fold. The disease has no impact on the muscular movement of the upper part of the face, such as knitting the brows and closing the eyes.

2) Peripheral Facial Paralysis

a. Patients often have the history of blockage of the facial nerve transmission, inflammation close to the ear, 2/3 hypogeusesthesia of the tongue, hyperacusis ... etc.

b. The disease often attacks the male patients between 20 to 50 years old.

c. The onset of disease is sudden, often early in the morning when patient just wakes up.

d. The paralysis, most often, is noticed in one side of the face. The main symptoms are pain inside the ear or on the mastoidea. disappearance of emotional expression on one side of the face, incomplete closure of the eye, lacrimation and failure to knit the brow ... etc.

e. There is hypomyotonia on the affected side of the face. The mouth corner is pulled to the healthy side. The nasolabial fold becomes shallow or deviated. The patients feel difficulty in speaking, blowing and pouting. There is also slobbering or such behavior as leaving food in the buccal cavity on the affected side.

f. Most cases will recover within 2 months after the onset.

g. Those with incomplete recovery may have facial muscular contracture, deviation of the mouth corner to the affected side perversion phenomenon, deepened nasolabial groove ... etc.

Acupuncture Treatment

Following is a brief introduction of the treatment of peripheral facial paralysis. For the treatment of central facial paralysis, please refer to the treatment of hemiplegia.

1) Filiform needle needling

Prescription 1

a. Point selection

Main points: Dicang (ST 4), Jiache (ST 6), Yangbai (GB 14), Sibai (ST 2), Hegu (LI 4)

Add Zanzhu (BL 2) for those who can not knit the brows. Add Yingxiang (LI 20) for shallowed nasolabial fold. Add Renzhong (DU 26) for deviation of the nasolabial fold. Add Yifeng (SJ 17) for pain in mastoid process. Add Chengjiang (RN 24) for deviation of the mentolabial sulcus. Add Lianquan (RN 23) for numbness of the tongue and hypogeusesthesia.

b. Manipulation

Except Hegu, all the above-mentioned points should be selected and needled in the affected side. For the main points, oblique needling or point-through-point needling should be performed, such as from Dicang to Jiache, from Yangbai to Yuyao (EX-HN 4), and from Sibai to Yingxiang. Moderate stimulation should be given, Or reducing method is adopted at the early stage of the treatment with the principle of shallow acupuncture with more needles. At the later stage of the treatment, reinforcing method is adopted.

c. Therapeutic course

One treatment is given everyday or every other day. 10 treatments constitute one therapeutic course.

Prescription 2

a. Point selection

Hegu (LI 4) and Taichong (LR 3) of both sides.

b. Manipulation

Patient in dorsal position and the points are needled perpendicularly. After deqi, retain the needles for 15 to 30 minutes, during which manipulate the needles 3 to 5 times.

c. Therapeutic course

One treatment is given everyday. 10 treatments constitute one therapeutic course.

Prescription 3

a. Point selection

Jiuzheng (on the ulnar side of the little finger, on the red-white muscle at the end of cross striation of the metacarpophalangeal joint)

b. Manipulation

Order the patient to clench the fist lightly and insert the needle from the lateral side of the hand, and along the anterior part of the metacarpal bone. Then penetrate it from Jiuzheng to Hegu.

c. Therapeutic course

One treatment is given everyday. 10 treatments constitute one therapeutic course. The spacing between two courses is 2 to 4 days.

2) Eye needling

a. Point selection

Shangjiao area, Liver-bladder area. Add Spleen-stomach area for insufficient vital qi.

b. Manipulation

The needle is inserted to the subcutaneous part along the edge of the orbit. The Shangjiao area is needled first, then the Liver-bladder area.

c. Therapeutic course

One treatment is given everyday. 10 treatments constitute one therapeutic course.

3) Ear acupuncture

a. Point selection

Eye, Cheek, Liver, Mouth, supported by Spleen, Forehead, Shenmen, Adrenal Gland.

b. Manipulation

During the early stage of the treatment, apply slight stimulation by filiform needling 3 to 5 ear points on the affected side in each treatment. Several days later, the filiform needle needling can be replaced by Electric therapy with low frequency impulse current or dense-sparse wave.

c. Therapeutic course

The treatment is given once everyday or every other day. When there is improvement, embedding of ear seeds may be used also. The seeds are changed once a week.

4) Electric therapy

a. Point selection

From Taiyang (KI 1) to Jiache (ST 6), from Jiache to Dicang (ST 4), from Yangbai (GB 14) to Yuyao (EX-HN 4)

Adjunct points: Hegu (LI 4), Yifeng (SJ 17)

b. Manipulation

Except Hegu that is needled in the healthy side, all the other points are on the affected side, When needling is applied from Taiyang to Jiache and from jiache to Dicang, a No. 28 filiform needle of 3 cun long is used for subcutaneous penetration. When needling is applied from Yangbai to Yuyao, a No. 30 filiform needle of 1.5 cun long is used. A G-6805 simulator is used to provide ever-increasing stimulation with either interrupted wave or dense-sparse wave for 15 to 30 minutes. For Hegu and Yifeng, there is no need to apply electric stimulation, but the needles should be retained for a similar length of time.

c. Therapeutic course

10 treatments constitute one therapeutic course. For the first five days, the treatment is given once everyday and for the later five days, once every other day. A spacing of 5 to 7 days should be arranged between 2 courses.

5) Needle warming through moxibustion

a. Point selection

Main points: Xiaguan (ST 7), Quanliao (SI 18)

Adjunct points: Jiache (ST 6), Dicang (ST 4), Taiyang (KI 1), Sibai (ST 2), Zanzhu (BL 2), Fengchi (GB 20), Hegu (LI 4), Yangbai (GB 14), Yingxiang (LI 20), Renzhong (DU 26), Chengjiang (RN 24), Qianzheng, Taichong (LR 3), Sanyinjiao (SP 6), Jianshi (PC 5)

b. Manipulation

For the main points, the uniform reinforcing and reducing should be performed to induce deqi. During the needles are retained, cast a moxa stick of 1 cun long to each of the needles. In each treatment, 1 to 2 moxa sticks are used until the local skin become reddish. 5 to 7 adjunct points can be selected alternatively in each treatment. Also the uniform reinforcing and reducing is performed.

c. Therapeutic course

The needling and moxibustion treatment can be given once everyday for the first 6 to 7 days. Then when there is improvement, treatment is given once every other day. 12 treatments constitute one therapeutic course. The spacing between two courses is 3 to 5 days.

6) Point injection

Prescription 1

a. Point selection

Tongziliao (GB 1), Xiaguan (ST 7), Jiache (ST 6) and Hegu (LI 4) on the healthy side

b. Manipulation

1 ml. of Vit. B_{12} solution (drug content: 15 to 50 μg) is injected in each point. For Tongziliao, Xiaguan and Jiache, oblique insertion should be conducted in the affected side, while for Hegu, perpendicular insertion is performed.

c. Therapeutic course

Two treatments every week. 6 treatments constitute one therapeutic course.

Prescription 2

a. Point selection

Taiyang (KI 1), Yangbai (GB 14), Sibai (ST 2), Qianzheng, Quanliao (LI 18), Yingxiang (LI 20), Jiache (ST 6), Daying (ST 5), Dicang (ST 4)

b. Manipulation

Divide the above points into three groups, and use each group in each treatment. First induce a soreness and distension sensation by lifting and thrusting, then inject 0.2 to 0.3 ml. of 0.4% Nitrate Securinine to each point.

c. Therapeutic course

One treatment is given everyday. 12 treatments constitute one therapeutic course. The spacing between two courses is 2 to 3 days.

7) Laser point irradiation

a. Point selection

Same as the Filiform needle needling

b. Manipulation

Use a He-Ne laser machine with an output of 3 mw to produce a light spot with a diameter of 2 mm on the point. In each treatment, 2 to 3 points are taken and each point is irradiated for 5 minutes.

c. Therapeutic course

One treatment is given everyday or every other day. 12 treatments constitute one therapeutic course. The spacing between two courses is 3 to 5 days.

8) Blood-letting puncture

Prescription 1

a. Point selection

(a) Jiache (ST 6)

(b) the ear tip or ear lobe

(c) small vein in the temple region

(d) zygomatic region

(e) Shangyang (LI 1)

b. Manipulation

The points both on the healthy and diseased sides will be taken alternatively.

(a) When Jiache is needled, tap the point 3 times with a fine three-edged needle and let out 1 to 3 ml. of blood by squeezing or cupping.

(b) Squeeze out 15 to 20 drops of blood after the ear tip or ear lobe is pricked with a fine cutting needle.

(c) First massage the minor veins in the temple area and then let out 3 ml. of blood by pricking with a fine three-edged needle.

(d) Prick Shangyang with a fine cutting needle and let out 10—20 drops of blood. Then let out 10 to 20 drops of blood from the small veins in the temporal region with the same method.

(e) Prick the zygomatic region twice with a thick cutting needle and let out 2 ml. of blood by means of cupping.

c. Therapeutic course

For those who are with a disease course of less than one

week, the treatment is given once or twice everyday. 7 treatments constitute one therapeutic course. The spacing between two courses is 3 to 5 days.

Prescription 2

a. Point selection

Dicang (ST 4), Jiache (ST 6), Yangbai (GB 14), Sibai (ST 2), Xiaguan (ST 7), Taiyang (KI 1), Yifeng (SJ 17), Heliao (LI 19)

b. Manipulation

Only the points of the affected side are needled. Tap the point until light petechiae occurs. Or cupping for 5 to 10 minutes is performed after tapping.

This therapeutic method is very effective to the paralysis in the inflammatory period and at the sequela stage when there is facial stiffness. Especially it is very effective to the "Perversion phenomenon".

c. Therapeutic course

One treatment is given every other day, 7 to 10 treatments constitute one therapeutic course.

9) Catgut implantation

a. Point selection

From 0. 5 cun of the lower part of the ear lobe to Jiache (ST 6), from Sibai (ST 2) to Quanliao (SI 18), from Dicang (ST 4) to Yingxiang (LI 20), from Yangbai (GB 14) to Touguangming

Adjunct points: Hegu (LI 4), Lieque (LU 7), Xuehai (SP 10)

b. Manipulation

According to the disease, select one pair of adjacent points and implant the fine catgut into the subcutaneous part of the points (local anesthesia is not needed). In each treatment, two remote points can be selected to support the therapeutic effect.

c. Therapeutic course

One treatment is given every 7 to 10 days. It is especially effective for long-standing cases.

10) Ginger moxibustion

a. Point selection

Same as Filiform needle needling

b. Manipulation

In each treatment, 3 to 5 points are needled. Cut the fresh ginger into slices of 0. 2 to 0. 4 cm thick and put the ginger slices on the selected points. Moxibustion the points with a moxa stick for 3 to 5 minutes in each treatment.

c. Therapeutic course

One treatment is given every day, 10 treatments constitute one therapeutic course.

11) Moxibustion through reed-pipe

a. Point selection

Inside the Auricle Canal.

b. Manipulation

Take a segment of reed-pipe with a diameter of 0. 4 to 0. 6 cm and a length of 5 to 6 cm. Make one end of the reed-pipe into duck-billed shape and seal the other end with adhesive plaster. This is known as one-segment reed moxibustion apparator. The two-segment reed moxibustion apparator is also made of reed-pipe. The length of the segment with duck-billed shape end is 4 cm and the diameter is 0. 8—1 cm. The length of the other segment which is to be inserted into the ear canal with mugwort floss is about 3 cm and the diameter is 0. 6—0. 8 cm. Join these two segments and a two-segment moxibustion apparator is ready.

During the moxibustion, first put the mugwort floss (With the size of half a peanut kernel) into the duck-billed shape end, burn it with thread incense, and then put the other end which is sealed with adhesive plaster into the ear canal until there is a warm-heat sensation in the ear, Generally the skin temperature should be made to raise 1 to 2 degrees. After the first moxa-cone is finished, change another one. In each treatment, 3 to 9 cones should be moxibustioned.

c. Therapeutic course

One treatment is given every day, 10 treatments constitute one therapeutic course.

12) Thunder-fire miraculous needle

a. Point selection

Dicang (ST 4), Jiache (ST 6), Xiaguan (ST 7), Yangbai (GB 14), Taiyang (KI 1) on the affected side.

b. Manipulation

This is a type of medicinal moxa roll made from 150 g of mugwort floss with eaglewood 3 g, costus root 3 g, notoptery-gium 3 g, cloves 3 g, frankincense 3 g, bark of Chinese cassia tree 3 g, turmeria 3 g, ledebouriella root 3 g, pangolin scales 3 g, and musk 0. 3 g.

Burn two thunder-fire miraculous needles simultaneously, and put 3 to 5 pieces of thick rough straw paper on top of the point. Press swiftly and heavily one of the needles on the point for 15 to 30 seconds. Then change the other thunder-fire needle quickly. Each point should be moxibustioned with above method for 3 to 5 times until the local skin becomes reddish.

c. Therapeutic course

The treatment is given once everyday. 12 treatments constitute one therapeutic course. The spacing between two courses is 3 to 5 days. During the second therapeutic course, the treatment is given once every other day.

13) The stiletto needle

a. Point selection

Mucous membrane of the mouth of the affected side.

For paralysis of the upper part of the face: the posterior area of the mucous membarnae (the opposite side of the great molar tooth)

For paralysis of the middle part of the face: the middle area of the mucous membrane (the opposite side of the small molar tooth)

For paralysis of the lower part of the face: the anterior, the anterosuperior and the anteroinferior areas of the mucous mem-branae (the superior and inferior part of the mouth corner on the opposite side of the lower canine tooth)

b. Manipulation

Incise an oblique incision of 0.1 to 0.3 cm deep and 1 to 1.5 cm long, massage and press the affected side with fingers, and scrape the incision with a tongue-spatula until the bleeding become bright-red. After the operation, cover the wound with cotton.

c. Therapeutic course

The treatment is given once everyday or every other day. For weak patients or patient with long duration, the treatment can be given once every 3 to 5 days.

14) Moxibustion with moxa cones

a. Point selection

Wangu (GB 12), Yifeng (SJ 17), the point under the ear lobe (about 0.3 cun below the connecting point between the ear lobe and the cheek)

b. Manipulation

For those with a disease course of less than half a month, moxibustion should be given as the main therapeutic method. During the treatment, moxibustion is applied under the ear lobe for 30 minutes. This treatment can be given twice a day. Meanwhile, Wangu or Yifeng can also be needled everyday or once every other day. When Wangu is needled, insert the needle to the direction of Yintang (EX-HN 3) for about 30 mm deep into the mastoid notch. When Yintang is needled, make the needle tip slightly upwards for 30 mm. When the point under the ear is needled, perpendicular insertion is performed for 15 mm, or oblique insertion is performed for 30 mm. Usually, bird-peck needling without twirling and rotating is performed on these points. But when the point under the ear lobe is needled obliquely, only twirling and rotating are performed. Retain the needle for 20 minutes. For those with a disease course of more than half a month, the needling should be taken as the main therapeutic method.

c. Therapeutic course

Same as above.

Therapeutic Effect

1) The author had obtained a very satisfactory result with acupuncture for the treatment of facial paralysis (refer to Typical Cases in Chapter Five). At the later stage of the needling treatment, moxibustion is often added.

2) dr, Liu Hongkui had treated 80 cases of facial paralysis with acupuncture. The point he selected is known as "Siguan" (namely bilateral elbow joints and knee joints). After an average treatment of 12 times. 71 cases were cured. 8 cases were improved and 1 case failed. (Journal of Heilongjiang TCM, 1989; 1)

3) Dr. Gao Yawei et al. reported 100 cases of facial paralysis treated with eye-acupuncture. As a result, 88 cases were cured and 12 cases remarkable improved. (Journal of Shaanxi TCM, 1989; 8:10)

Dr. Li Zhiming treated 117 cases with Needle warming through moxibustion. The results showed that the total effective rate was 100% (76.9% were cured). He also treated 74 cases with Reed-pipe moxibustion. The total effective rate was 98.65%. (Journal of Chinese Acupuncture, 1987; 2:7)

Discussion

1) Dr. Guo Xiaozong states that when needling is used to treat this disorder, five different manipulating methods can be selected, namely: soothing, clearing, warming, reinforcing and reducing. The treatment should be given according to the physical conditions of the patient. For example, to those with neither excess nor deficiency, the soothing (uniform reinforcing and reducing) method is used. For those with deficiency, reinforcing method is often applied. For those with excess, reducing method is often adopted. For those with excess caused by external pathogenic factors, clearing method is taken, and for those with obstruction caused by external pathogenic factors, warming

method is employed. In the acute stage of the disease, generally reducing and clearing method are used, while in the recovery stage, the warming and reinforcing are used, For points on the healthy side, heavy needling is made and for points on the affected side, light needling is performed. (Journal of TCM, 1988; 4: 29)

2) Dr. Chen Keqin considered that the key points in treating this disease were:

a. Timely treatment i. e. the earlier the treatment, the better the results. A delayed treatment may result in more sequelae.

b. The number of points to be needled should be planned properly.

c. A well-selected therapeutic manipulation should be used.

d. In the course of treatment the face should be protected from pathogenic wind-cold. In addition, massage on the affected area is essential to raise the therapeutic effect.

3) In the past, there was much controversy about the application of acupuncture, especially the electric therapy in the treatment of facial paralysis in acute stage. The study of Dr. Tang Xianli, pointed out that the facial nerve is in a state of parabiosis when the paralysis occurs in acute stage. If a very mild benign stimulation is given at this moment to excite the nerves, it can help increase the contraction of the muscle fiber, improve the blood circulation, metabolism and absorption of the inflammatory exudate, so that the transmission of nerve impulse can be improved and the regeneration of the nerve fiber can be accelerated. As a result, the nerve function can be restored. Most often the dense-sparse wave and the continuous wave are selected. The roles played by this kind of current are to excite the nerve and the muscular tissues, to improve the blood circulation and nutrition, accelerate the absorption of the exudate and to prolong the time when the affected muscle become atrophied and degenerated. Therefore, the facial paralysis in the acute stage can be needled with acupuncture or electric therapy with very solid scientif-

ic basis. (Journal of Chinese Acupuncture, 1987; 5:7)

4) Advice the patient to take good care of the eye that is not able to close. Use an eye mask if necessary. To support the treatment wet-hot compress, massage or ultra-red ray radiation can be used.

5) Stiletto needling is contraindicated in pregnancy and in patients with purpura and anemia. In the treatment with point injection, there may be individual cases with local swelling, which may disappear spontaneously with the decrease or withdrawal of the drugs.

6) For central facial paralysis, Fengchi, Baihui and Fengfu can be added in the needling treatment. If scalp acupuncture is used, lower 2/5 of Dingnie Qianxiexian and Nieqianxian is often taken. During needling and retaining of needle, massage on the affected part should be performed until the local skin becomes reddish.

CHAPTER FOUR
THE OTHER SUPPLEMENTARY
TREATMENTS

In the acupuncture treatment of paralysis, besides the treatment based on the symptoms and the etiology, the accessory treatment is also essential.

SECTION I
Physical Training for Rehabilitation

Taking medical treatment as the goal, the dirigation is a kind of active functional exercise and an important measure for the patient with paralysis to recover. In ancient times, this was called "Daoyin" a term referring to physical and breathing exercises combined with auto-massage.

In practicing functional exercises, the patients are required to enhance their conscious training and movement guided by the conscious activities. Efforts should be made to encourage the patient to participate in the struggle against their own diseases, and to set up a firm believe of recovering the health.

The functional exercise can not only exert a direct effect on the muscles and joints of the affected part, it can also influence the functions of internal organs in a reflective manner, improving the pathophysiologic process and accelerating the recovery of the limb functions. Furthermore, the patient with paralysis may suffer from hypofunction, functional disturbance or even loss of the functions in some organs or tissues. Functional exercise can improve the functions of the diseased organs and raise the compensatory ability.

The functional exercise in the needling treatment can also help dredge the meridian and promote the qi-blood circulation. As the patient is asked to concentrate the mind on the "movable" affected part, it is easier to achieve "bringing qi to the diseased site" and to get rid of the pathogenic factors.

1. Methods of Physical Training

There are various kind of functional exercises, all of which have a common goal, i.e. to recover the functions of the paralysed limb. The exercises can be conducted during the needling or retaining of needle, or they can be conducted separately. They can be done bare-handedly or with the support of convalescent apparatus.

1) Conscious training

In conducting conscious exercise, the patient must overcome all the external interference and concentrate his mind on the affected limbs. It is required that the conscious activity of the patient could direct his own limb movement.

a. The combination of the conscious activity and passive movement: The so-called passive movement is actually an exercise during which the doctor helps the patient to move his affected limb from the proximal end to the distal end and to move his joints. The amplitude of the movement is gradually from small to large so as to avoid further injury. Meanwhile, the patient should try his best to carry out all the movements consciously under the guidance of doctor.

b. The combination of the conscious activity and the exercise of the healthy limb: Firstly, the patient should have a firm consciousness to direct various movements of his healthy limb under the guidance of doctor. The doctor may ask the patient to move the affected limb repeatedly or repeat the same movement alternatively with his healthy and the affected limbs.

c. Treatment with consciousness: The doctor should help the patient establish an ability of imagination, through which the patient can assume that his disorder had been cured, and his limb was able to perform different kind of activities, so that the active movement of the affected limb can be promoted. Dr. Zhang Liangshan, for example, had cured 3 cases of paraplegia with this method. During the treatment, he taught the patient to imagine that he had recovered from the disease. Meanwhile he performed an integrated therapeutic method of qigong, digital point pressure and herbal medicine. At the time when the patient did not receive the treatment, he directed the patient to practice conscious imagination. For example, the patient could assume that his big toe moved first, followed by the rest toes or that his leg could be lifted ⋯ etc. (Journal of Qigong, 1987; 9:8)

2) Simple movement exercises

The doctor should encourage the patient to practice such simple movements with his affected limb as stretching, bending, rubbing, kneading, raising, unfolding, stamping, kicking, sitting down and standing up. These movements should be performed repeatedly by the patient under the order of the doctor, who will plan the time of the exercise according to the actual conditions of the patient and the goal of the exercises. For example, when the patient is ordered to bend and stretch out his finger 50 times, the doctor can give orders in a rhythmical manner. Again, when the patient is practicing standing up and sitting domn for 20 times, the doctor can count the numbers, and at the same time, encourage the patient to finish all the required movements.

3) Therapeutic walking

With the improvement of the myodynamia, the patient with paralysis of the lower limbs should begin to practice walking under the help of other people or by himself. This kind of walking must be with a therapeutic purpose. For example, there is often weakened myodynamia in the flexor and adductor of the patient's paralysed lower limb. Therefore the patient, while practicing the therapeutic walking, should be directed to practice bending of the hip, knees and raising of the leg repeatedly.

The speed, distance, slope, and duration of the walking

should be determined and adjusted according to the conditions of the patient.

The walking must be carried out under the supervision of the doctor who should provide the essentials and guidance, and correct every possible mistake as soon as it occurs. Such unhealthy walking shape as abduction or extorsion, which occurs very commonly in patient with paraplegia, must be corrected. For example, stretching out the foot, lifting the foot, raising the toes ⋯ etc should be encouraged in guiding the walking for patient with injury of common peroneal nerve.

During the exercise, it is advisable that no walking aid should be used, such as a walking stick or the crutches, lest the patient will become dependent and the paralysed limb can not be recovered easily. Therefore the patient should be encouraged to walk with his own effort. For those who can not, they should practice walking with the help of their upper limbs.

4) Load carrying exercise

Load carrying exercise plays an important role in improving and increasing the myodynamia. It is known also as "progressive resistance exercise".

The doctor who directs this kind of exercises must know very well about the normal functions of every muscle group of the body. When the diagnosis of paralysis is determined, a certain weight can be given on the distal end of the paralysed muscle group. Then the patient is ordered to repeat some movement. For example, in training the musculus quadriceps femoris, as it belongs to the muscle group that is responsible for stretching the knee and bending the hip, a sand bag or some other object with proper weight can be bound to the small leg. Then the patient is ordered to practice knee-stretching in a sitting position or hip-bending in a lying position.

5) Exercise with convalescent apparatus

There are different kind of convalescent apparatus available in the market. People can also make them by themselves. The convalescent apparatus can be used to help recover the function of the diseased part such as the joints, the upper and lower limbs by the active movement of the patient. According to the specific aim of each kind, patient can select one or several kind for the functional exercises. Self-made convalescent apparatus must be designed according to the nature and location of the paralysis. Attention should be paid to the safety and effort is made to prevent from accidents.

6) Medical exercises

when the disease is recovered to a certain degree, patient with paralysis can begin to learn different kind of medical exercises to accelerate the recovery. The most common medical exercises include: Taijiquan (the five mimic-animal boxing), Yiji Jing (12-form sinew transforming exercise), Liuduan Jing (brocade exercise in 6-forms) ⋯ etc.

7) Passive exercises

For those who can not perform active movement, passive exercises with special aims are encouraged besides the conscious exercise. This kind of exercises can be carried out under the help of the doctor or the family members. Sometimes the patient can also conduct some kind of passive exercise by himself. This kind of exercises range from helping the patient to move certain part of the body to providing certain kind of therapeutic methods such as massage or rubbing.

a. Pressing: Press rhythmically with fingers or the palm on the skin or points of the patient.

b. Rubbing: Rub the affected skin or points of the patient with the fingers or palm of the operator.

c. Pushing: Push and squeeze the affected muscles forcefully with the fingers or palm to different directions.

d. Grasping: Lift and squeeze or lift and release the affected muscles with one or both hands of the operator.

e. Kneading: Press and move a meridian point or the diseased part to and fro with the fingers or palm.

f. Foulaging: Knead and press the affected limb or muscles with one or both hands.

g. Finger-nail pressing: Press forcefully at a point with a finger-nail.

h. Digital point-pressing: Press forcefully at a point with one finger.

i. Tapping: Tap the body and extremities with the palm or fist.

Please refer to Chapter Three for selection of points in the massage and rubbing movement.

2. Conditions and Duration of the Physical Training for Rehabilitation

1) Conditions of the functional exercises

It is stressed that early functional exercise should given to the patient for better recovery. The presence of paralysis does not mean that there is already muscular atrophy or joint deformity. If an early acupuncture treatment plus functional exercise can be conducted at this moment, it is easy to make the paralysed limb recover. On the contrary, most bedridden patients are inevitable to suffer from joint deformity and muscular atrophy, and complicated with bed-sore, hypostatic pneumonia or impairment of qi, general weakness, constipation, poor appetite ··· etc.

Generally speaking, the functional exercises should start as soon as the vital signs become stable. This will cause no worries to most of the patients with paralysis except those with cerebral hemorrhage. What they are afraid of is "rehemorrhage" which endangers their lives. As a matter of fact, such worries are groundless. Recent study reveals the rate of rehemorrage is only about 2%, and the earliest recorded rehemorrhage occurred two months later after the first attack. These two factors should be enough to encourage the patient to practice early exercises.

2) Duration of the functional exercises

In each exercise, the duration is arranged between 20 to 30 minutes. Usually after the exercises, the patient feels a bit tired or there is mild soreness and pain in the affected limb. However, the patient will get rid of the above discomfort after a rest for half a day or so. The amount of exercise should not be too great to exceed the tolerance of the patient, otherwise the exercise can not reach the expected aim or cause harmful consequences.

The total amount of the exercise within a day, generally, should be no less than 2 hours. But during the time when there is not functional exercise, too much lying in bed is not advisable, because it would cause "impairment of qi due to long staying in bed".

3. Points for Attention in Physical Training for Rehabilitation

1) functional exercises must be carried out under the guidance and supervision of a medical personnel. First of all, the essentials and aims of the exercise should be made clear and any incorrect movement must be corrected immediately. Meanwhile, any independent movement of the patient should be avoided to prevent from accidents.

2) The exercise can be carried out from simple movements gradually to difficult ones. The time and amount of exercise should be increased gradually. Try to plan the exercise in orderly way and any impatience in treatment should be avoided.

3) The doctor must be fine enough to find out or encourage every progress made by the patient. Whenever there is any disappointment in the patient during treatment, the doctor should help the patient to overcome it and to carry on the exercise through to the end.

4) Attention should be paid to avoid overfatigue of the patient due to too much exercise, and observe carefully the changes of the pulse, respiration, blood pressure ⋯ etc.

SECTION II
Psychotherapy

In traditional Chinese medicine, psychotherapy is also called "emotional treatment". In a broad sense, the psychotherapy includes the improvement of the environment, the spoken skills of the surrounding people (including the doctor), specific decoration and arrangement of a therapeutic environment, the technology of psychological treatment of the doctor. In a narrow sense, it refers mainly to the technology of the doctor's psychological treatment which include persuasion, suggestion therapy, psychoanalysis, behavior therapy, biofeedback therapy, Qigong therapy, Yujia therapy, physiotherapy or music therapy and so on.

In the psychological treatment, a doctor should influence and change the feelings, recognitions, attitudes and behaviors of the patient through his own language, emotions, gestures and movements so that the sufferings and various kind of nervous factors of the patients can be relieved. Some passive attitude and abnormal behavior of the patient can be eliminated and some symptoms can be improved. This therapy is effective not only to those with hysterical paralysis, but also to any patients in any age group who are willing to receive the treatment.

1. The Harmful States of Mind and Their Impact on the Recovery

Before and after the appearance of paralysis, the patients may develop various kind of unhealthy psychological activities which are unfavorable to the recovery of the disease, along with the changes of their status in the society and in the family. They include:

1) Loss of confidence

Some patients with hemiplegia, or paraplegia, or quadriplegia may have the idea that they are suffering from an "incurable disease". Therefore, they become disappointed and listless, or even collapsed. It is not easy for them to accept the treatment or to cooperate in the treatment.

2) Eager to be cured

This kind of patients wish that the disease could be cured in one minute. They lack the moral preparation to have a long term treatment against the disease. They may become suspicious to the treatment and hypercritical to the nursing. When their needs can not be satisfied, they are easy to loss their confidence.

3) Horror

The patients think that their disease may kill them at any moment, and any acupuncture treatment or functional exercise may aggravate the disease or even endanger their lives.

4) Dependence

This kind of patients have a very strong idea dependent on the drugs, especially on the rare and expensive medicinal herbs, but they don't want to practice active functional exercises.

The unhealthy attitudes as mentioned above can cause a more serious and harmful effect to the body than the paralysis in their limbs. The spiritual disappointment and horror may lead to functional disturbance, obstruction of qi-blood circulation and other discomfort and symptoms in the body. On the other hand, the emotional instability may result in aggravation of the disease, especially for those with cerebrovascular accident. Sometimes, this may induce a second attack of the disease. Lastly, the unhealthy attitude may prolong the disease course or loss the chance of a timely treatment.

2. Methods of the Psychotherapy

According to the therapeutic form, the psychotherapy can be divided into individual, collective, and family psychotherapies. According to the therapeutic contents, it can be divided into persuasion therapy, education therapy, hypnotherapy, suggestion therapy, analytic psychotherapy, music or art therapy, frame therapy, kinesitherapy, and static therapy. A brief introduction to some of the therapeutic methods is as follows.

1) Persuasion method

Efforts should be made to make persuasion, explanation, straightening or exhortation. Try to rid the patients of their worries, burdens and the pessimistic attitude towards the disease, and help the patients set up a confidence to win over the disease. Through the efforts, divert the patients' attention and free their mind of apprehensions. This therapeutic method can help regulate the functional activities of qi, improve the disturbance of qi-blood circulation and stabilize the emotions of the patients. For example certain critical cases with satisfactory results in very short therapeutic course can be cited to persuade the patient. Some new advances or new achievements in the treatment of this disease can be used to encourage the patient. For example, the new concept of "Human spinal cord can regenerate under certain conditions and the functions of the nervous system can be restored after injury of spinal cord" is a very good inspiration to the paralysed patients. It is often used to help the patient change their own pathological state, and has played an active role in the acupuncture treatment.

2) Emotional stimulation method

The emotion activities belong respectively to the Five Zang organs. Different emotional change can cause different changes in functional activities of qi in Zang-Fu. Under the pathological conditions, try to induce a kind of emotional activity and use it to correct the qi-blood disturbance caused by over-excitative emotion. This method is very similar to the modern behavior correction therapy. For example, to those who have lost confidence in the disease and do not want to conduct any functional exercise (This kind of patients often lie in bed with few words and little facial expression.), we can try to "enrage" them by saying "Somebody has been better through the exercises. He behaves much better than you". With this method, we can help the patient get rid of the unhealthy distracting thoughts and get out off the bed to practice exercises.

3) Suggestion therapy

This therapeutic method can be used either singly or together with other methods. The suggestion therapy is divided into the self-suggestion and the suggestion by others. The latter is a method with which the one who provides the suggestion should pass his views to the patient so that the views can work in the consciousness or in the subconsciousness of the patient. This therapeutic method can also be applied together with persuasion or other methods. Meanwhile, according to the emotional conditions, the doctor can teach the patient the method of selfsuggestion, with which the patient is able to regulate his emotions and relieve his own tonicity and excitement. No matter which kind of suggestion is used, it can improve the psychological state of the patient and the physiological functions of the body, and raise the therapeutic effect of the acupuncture therapy.

4) Self-regulation and self-training

Based on a set of specific procedures, this is a kind of behavior therapy, utilizing one reaction of the body to modify another reaction of the body. Clinically the most common method is to teach the patient some basic and simplest Qigong, such as the qigong for relax, the qigong for getting stronger, and the qigong for regulation qi. The relaxation and quiescence thus produced by qigong may lower the tonicity and excitement and stabilize the emotion of the patient.

3. Points for Attention in Psychotherapy

1) The focus of the psychotherapy is the human body as a whole, rather than a limited area or part of the body. It is a therapeutic method concentrated on the etiology rather than the morbid state of the body. Therefore we have to regulate the whole body and even the environment and make the body as a harmonious whole. Only in this way can we eliminate the abnormal states both in the mentality and in the body and take an active part in the acupuncture treatment.

2) In psychological treatment, the doctor should understand fully the disease conditions, the diagnosis, what is more, the past history, characteristics, interest and self-cultivations of each individual patient before he starts to treat the patients. This is the only way to ensure a satisfactory effect.

3) During the treatment, the patient should be encouraged to give full initiatives and cooperate in the acupuncture treatment. The doctor is a friend rather than an educator of the patient. Meanwhile, the authoritativeness of the doctor should not

be stressed too much. Efforts should be made to lessen the dependence of the patient on the doctor.

SECTION III
Accessory Acupuncture Treatment at Home

After the acute stage, most of the patients with paralysis will be back home to receive further acupuncture treatment for rehabilitation. The acupuncturists can also visit the patient at his home. During this period of time, some simple therapeutic methods can be applied at home so as to raise the effect and to accelerate the recovery.

1. Acupoint Irradiation with Ultra-Red Ray

The ultra-red ray can play an important role in improving the blood circulation and cellular functions, and ameliorating the pain and muscle spasm. It can relieve the muscular paralysis, atrophy and spasm of the limbs, and contracture of the joints. Ultra-red ray irradiation therapy at home can help increase the therapeutic effect of the acupuncture treatment.

In each treatment, irradiate the point or point area for 20 to 30 minutes. The distance between the lamp and the skin is about 30 to 50 cm. The doctor can adjust the electric power until there are evenly-distributed pink spots on the local skin and a warmth sensation felt by the patient. The treatment can be given twice a day.

Cautions should be taken to prevent from burning the skin especially for those with sensory disturbance, and to avoid a direct irradiation on the eyes. The patient should be watched to avoid the signs of post-irradiative tiredness, insomnia, dizziness ··· etc. If the side-reaction is too great, the irradiation can be stopped. This therapeutic method is not applicable to those patients with severe arteriosclerosis, or with heart failure, hemorrhagic tendency as well as those with high fever. Usually the ultra-red ray lamp is available in the market.

2. Magnetotherapy on Acupoint

The electromagnetic wave provokes resonance of the basic particles of the human body and induce thermal and biochemical effects in the diseased sites. It can also regulate the human bio-electric field and improve the disease conditions. Especially it can help decrease the swelling and inflammation, stop the pain and improve the microcirculation, promote metabolism, strengthen the recovery and regeneration of the local tissues in the affected limbs, muscles and in the injured nerves and joints.

Put the bare diseased part or the Jingluo points under the electromagnetic apparatus with a distance of about 15—25 cm. It is required that a warmth sensation can be felt and pink spots can be noticed in the local skin. Usually the temperature of the skin under irradiation is no more than 45 ℃. The time of irradiation is between 30 and 40 minutes. The treatment is usually given twice daily. Six to eight days' treatment consists of one therapeutic course. The spacing between two courses is 3 to 5 days.

As mentioned in ultra-red ray irradiation, the same cautions should also be taken in this therapeutic method.

3. Mild Moxibustion

The mild moxibustion is a kind of moxibustion which include mugwort stick moxibustion, moxibustion with moxibustioner, the ironing moxibustion and the sunlight moxibustion. A brief introduction is as follows.

1) Moxibustion with a mugwort stick

Burn one end of the mugwort stick and place this end 2 to 3 cm above the point. Maintain the treatment for 10 to 15 minutes or even longer.

If the burning mugwort stick is waved over the point forwards and backwards and right or left, this is known as waving moxibustion.

The sparrow-pecking moxibustion is another moxibustion technique --- to touch swiftly a point with a burning mugwort stick like a bird-pecking. The distance between the stick and the skin is about 2 cm. Each point can be moxibustioned for 5 to 10 minutes until local redness of the skin. 1 to 3 points can be moxibustioned in each treatment.

The above-mentioned moxibustion techniques can motivate the qi-blood circulation, warm the meridians to eliminate pathogenic cold and keep the body in a sound condition. It can improve the disease conditions both locally and systematically.

2) Moxibustion with a moxibustioner

A rectangle wood box is specially made with the plate of 0. 5 cm thick. The box has no bottom but instead an iron gauze is fixed there 3 to 4 cm above the bottom edges. During the treatment, put a burning mugwort stick in the box which is placed on top of a selected point for 15 to 30 minutes. It is effective for muscular atrophy or contracture of joint. The cover of the box is free to open and close so that the temperature inside can be regulated. The iron gauze is used to hold the ashes of the burned mugwort. Several adjacent points can be treated in one moxibustion treatment.

3) The ironing moxibustion

First place some mugwort floss on the point or the affected area. Then cover a piece of cloth on top of the floss. Iron the cloth surface to and fro with an electric iron or a cup of hot water to induce warm sensation in the local skin. This therapeutic method is good for pain or muscular atrophy.

4) Sunlight Moxibustion

Put the mugwort floss on the point or the affected part and then exposed to strong sunlight for 20 to 30 minutes. Care should be taken to prevent from sun-stroke. The normal skin should also be protected properly.

This method is also good for pain, muscular atrophy or contraction of the affected limb.

4. Massage

Massage, as well as the magnetic rubber hammer can all be

used to relieve the muscular atrophy and spasm through their effect of massage, rubbing and point-pressing. They can help promote the local blood flow and the nutritions of the local tissues. They can also warm the meridians and collaterals, dissipate the blood stasis to stop the pain, promote the qi-blood circulation and improve such sensory disturbance in the limb as numbness, cold-pain, soreness and heaviness.

5. Acupuncture with Magnetic Needle

The magnetic needle which looks like a ball-ben is a new type of acupuncture needle. It is made according to the ancient theory of "Nine Needles" and modern "magnetic field therapy". Both the patient and his family members can use it easily at home. During the treatment, the points can be selected locally, or the pain spots can be taken as Shu points. In each treatment, 2 to 3 points can be needled. Press the needle body vertically against the skin surface for 10 to 20 minutes. The treatment is given once daily.

There are many accessory acupuncture methods which can be used at home. Anyone of them which is good for the recovery of the disease can be adopted.

CHAPTER FIVE
ANALYSIS OF TYPICAL CASES

1. Cerebrovascular Accident

Mrs. Liu, a farmer of 81 years old, first visited the doctor on 6 May 1986.

In the night of 1 May 1986 when the patient got up for urination, she was found to suffer from a sudden aphasia and paraplegia in her left lower limb. She was taken to the hospital next morning. Examination revealed that the patient had a clear mind. But there was shallowed nasolabial fold, aphasia, 0 degree of the myodynamia in the muscles of the right upper limb and the right lower limb. Therefore a diagnosed of cerebral thrombosis with hemiplegia of the right side was made. Treatment consisted of scalp needling on Ezhongxian, Dingzhongxian and DingnieQianxiexian (right) with "qi withdrawal", method were carried out. Meanwhile the limb exercises was encouraged to reinforce the needling treatment. Following the first treatment, the patient could speak some simple words and she could also stand up and walk a little under the help of other people. After 3 day's treatment, she could walk for half a kilometer by herself, but with titubation. After a continuous treatment for 15 days, the patient recovered completely. No relapse observed in the follow-up period.

Note: In this case, the cerebral thrombosis is the main cause for the hemiplegia of the right limbs and the aphasia. The scalp acupuncture on Dingnie Qianxiexian and Dingzhongxian can help the patient gain the myodynamia in the affected limbs and correct the hemiplegia due to the "wind-stroke". Needling

Ezhongxian has the effect of relieving mental stress. It can also correct the anandia. This therapeutic method has been found to have very good effect on the sequelae of hemiplegia due to cerebral embolism and cerebral hemorrhage.

2. Post-Hemiplegic Syndrome

Mrs. Cai, a 64-year-old farmer, complained of sudden onset of hemiplegia in her left limbs, deviation of the eyes and mouth and difficulty in speaking when she got up in the morning of 27 August 1985 (The Chinese Lunar Calendar). She was diagnosed as cerebral thrombosis with hemiplegia of the left side. After a treatment with both Western or herbal medicine for over 8 months, she still was bedridden and could not move her left limbs. The mouth corner deviated to the right with salivation. Then she consulted our hospital of acupuncture treatment.

Examination revealed that the patient was fatty with clear mind and normal blood pressure. There were nasolabial fold shallowed in the left side, slight deviation of the mouth corner and some difficulty in speaking. She could not stand or sit because there was weakness in the lower limbs. The myodynamia for both left upper and lower limbs were of grade II with slight muscular atrophy. Then scalp acupuncture was performed with Dingzhongxian and Zhenshang Zhengzhongxian as the main needling lines. To strengthen the therapeutic effect, she was also encouraged to practice swallowing movement and language drills. Then the upper 1/5 of Dingnie Qianxiexian and middle 2/5 of Dingnie Qianxiexian were needled with proper limb exercises. During the needling, the method of "qi withdrawal" was adopted. After the treatment, the patient could sit by herself and perform certain simple movement of the affected lower limb, such as raising the leg and stamping the foot. The affected upper limb could raise to touch the third button. She could also stand for a short period of time. Then the needles were retained for 24 hours. The treatment was given daily for 10 days as therapeutic course.

After the first therapeutic course, the patient could already walk by herself and raise her upper limb to the shoulder, the facial paralysis alleviated and the spoken ability returned. However, there were still slight strephenopodia and difficulty in the movement of the fingers. Then the patient was ordered to have a rest for 10 days before the start of the second therapeutic course.

In the second therapeutic course, the scalp needling and the body needling were given alternately. For the scalp needling, same needling lines were selected, and for the filiform needling Jianliao (SJ 14), Jianyu (LI 15), Binao (LI 14), Quchi (LI 11), Waiguan (SJ 5), Hegu (LI 4); Huantiao (GB 30), Futu (ST 32), Liangqiu (ST 34), Yanglingquan (GB 34), Zusanli (ST 36), Jueneifan, Xuanzhong (GB 39), Qiuxu (GB 40) were selected. In each treatment, 4 points respectively from both the upper and lower limbs were selected. A G-6805 stimulator was used for 15 to 20 minutes with continuous wave. As mentioned above, the patient was treated five times and was cured on the whole. A follow-up of 4 years found that the patient was completely cured with no relapse. She could manage all her housework and walk for more than 5 kilometers.

Note: If the needling treatment can be given immediately after the central symptoms become stable, the patient with paralysis due to wind-stroke can usually be recovered 1 to 3 months after the onset. However, satisfactory therapeutic effect can also be obtained to those with a longer disease course. This case had been confined in bed for over 8 months, but she was cured after two courses of treatment. This indicates that acupuncture is very effective to the paralysis.

3. Cerebral Injury with Paralysis of the Lower Limb

Mr. Xu, a farmer of 48 years old, fell into a pit of 4—5 meters deep, hurting his head with temporary loss of consciousness. There was bleeding in the left ear and the nose. He could not move his right lower limb. In addition, he also had headache, nausea, and vomiting. He was sent to our hospital two days later.

Examination revealed that the patient was clear in the mind and cooperative. The temperature was 37°C, pulse: 77 times/minute, respiration: 18 times/minute, blood pressure: 126/72 mm Hg, left pupil: 0. 35 cm and right pupil 0. 3 cm both with reflex to the light, normal myodynamia in both upper limbs, but poor sensory sensation in the skin of the right lower limb, myodynamia: grade II, the patellar tendon reflex: ↑, and babinski's sign and Kernig's sign: (-). There was drop of the right ankle joint. The skull X-ray film shows basicranial fracture. The patient was diagnosed as (a) basicranial fracture, (b) concussion of the brain and (c) cerebral trauma complicated with incomplete paralysis of the right lower limb. A consultation was then organized with the presence of some acupuncturists. When the patient was examined again, it was found that there was no wound on the scalp and there was pink liquid running out from the left ear. All the rest symptoms and signs were the same as mentioned above. Then the penetration needling was performed on Dingzhongxian and upper 1/5 of Dingnie Qianxiexian (left) with the method of "qi withdrawal". Immediately after the needling, the patient could raise her right lower limb and the myodynamia increased to grade III. This therapeutic method was given once daily for 3 days when the patient could get off the bed and walk in titubation. Then the treatment was given every other day. After a therapeutic course of ten treatments, the patient found his myodynamia and skin sensory sensation normal again.

Note: This case is the kind of paralysis caused by cerebral trauma whose pathogenesis is different from that of the cerebrovascular accident. However needling Dingnie Qianxiexian can achieve marked immediate therapeutic effect. Only after ten treatments, the patient was cured and discharged from the hospital. If there is scalp wound on the opposite side of the paralysed limb, same satisfactory therapeutic effect can also be obtained by needling same-side Dingnie Qianxiexian.

4. High Paraplegia

Mr. Zhao, a farmer of 57 years old, first visited the hospital on 25 May 1986.

The neck of patient was accidently hit by a falling tree branch on 1 February 1985 when he was putting off a fire. Then he began to feel numbness of both lower limbs and the four limbs failed to move. He was taken to a hospital for emergency treatment. Examination showed that the mentality was clear. Both pupils were of the same size with normal light reflex. The cranial nerves were normal; burn of grade II on the left forehead was noted. The myodynamia of both upper and lower limbs: 0 degree. X-ray films of cervical vertebrae showed no bone fracture or dislocation, but the physiological curvature below the fourth cervical vertebra is abnormal with a difference of 1—2 mm. The patient was diagnosed as (a) injury of the cervical spinal cord (b) burn in the head. During hospitalization, the patient received skull traction, antibiotics and symptomatic treatment. 48 days later, both upper limbs and the fingers still could not move with disappearance of sensation. The myodynamia of both lower limbs was grade II, but he could not stand up. The patient also suffered from constipation and difficulty in urination. Then the patient was treated with herbal medicine until he came for help to the acupuncture department of the hospital. Based on the new diagnosis of high paraplegia, 3 groups of points were taken and needled alternatively. They are: Huatuojiaji points along side the cervical vertebrae, Fengchi (GB 20), Jianyu (LI 15), Quchi (LI 11), Zhongzhu (SJ 3), Yangchi (SJ 4), Waiguan (SJ 5), Hegu (LI 4); Shenshu (BL 23), Mingmen (DU 4), Pangguangshu (BL 28), Dachangshu (BL 25), Ciliao (BL 32), Huantiao (GB 30), Zhibian (BL 54), Yinmen (BL 37), Chengfu (BL 36), Fengshi (GB 31), Weizhong (BL 40), Zusanli (ST 36), Yanglingquan (GB 34), Chengshan (BL 57), Sanyinjiao (SP 6), Kunlun (BL 60), Qiuxu (GB 40); and Guanyuan (RN 4), Qihai (RN 6), Zhongji (RN 3), Tianshu (ST 25). In the treatment 4 points from the upper limb and 4 from the lower limb were selected and connected to a G-6805 stimulator. The continuous wave was used for 15 to 20 minutes. Meanwhile, the scalp acupuncture was also adopted by needling Dingzhongxian, Dingnie Qianxiexian and Dingnie Houxiexian with the method of "qi withdrawal". the needles were retained for 24 hours and active and passive functional exercises were arranged. The treatment was given once every other day. 10 treatments constitute one therapeutic course.

After 4 to 5 therapeutic courses, the patient could walk with improved myodynamia, but the walking was not stable. His hip joint, knee joint and ankle joint could flex or extend very well, so could the joints in the shoulder and elbow. However, the constipation was not improved and the sensory disturbance still existed. After that, the patient insisted on practicing functional exercises at home. By 1991 when a follow-up was made, the patient was found to be able to lift a weight of 7.5 Kg with the upper limb and to walk for 5 km by himself. He had defecation once every 6 to 7 days. The sensory sensation of the fingers, toes and the soles was still not very well recovered.

Note: This is a case of high paraplegia caused by the injury of the cervical spinal cord. According to TCM theory, it belongs to injury of Du Meridian. The obstruction of the meridian and the sudden stagnancy of qi-blood circulation deprive the nutrients of the four limbs, and cause their paralysis. Needling Dingzhongxian and Huatoujiaji points alongside the cervical vertebrae can activate the primordial energy in the Du Meridian. Needling the Shu points on the back and the points on the four limbs, as well as Dingnie Qianxiexian and Dingnie Houxiexian can improve the motor and sensory functions of the limbs. Together with the active and passive functional exercises, the needling therapy is very effective.

5. Polyneuritis

Mr. Xu was a student of 16 years old. He was admitted to

the hospital on 10 July 1985 because of irregular movements of four limbs in seeing a cinema. When asked about the reasons, the patient answered that he had noticed numbness and distension in the limbs for several days.

Physical examination disclosed formication sensation, gloveanesthesia, or sock-anesthesia and sometimes burning pain in the affected limbs. There was a thickness sensation in the palms and soles. A diagnosed of multiple neuritis was made. Filiform needle needling was prescribed. The points selected were Quchi (LI 11), Waiguan (SJ 5), Baxie; Zusanli (ST 36), Sanyinjiao (SP 6), Bafeng (EX-LE 10). Moderate stimulation was induced by lifting, thrusting, twirling and rotating. The first five treatments were given once everyday, and the later five were given once every other day. Electric therapy with a G-6805 stimulator was given for 15 to 20 minutes. The patient was asked to increase nutrition and to perform functional exercises of the affected limbs. The patient was cured by one course of treatment.

Note: As the patient was a weak and slim man, it was considered that his disease was due to poor nutrition. He was cured only with one therapeutic course because his symptoms were mild and were found fairly early. In addition, the patient was young. The authors saw quite a few cases of this kind, but most of them were caused by poisoning, such as sulfa-drugs, isoniazid, organic phosphorus and so on. Those who have a prolonged disease course or who are seriously poisoned are difficult to cure. Even those who have obtained immediate therapeutic effect may have relapse. Therefore an early and timely treatment can assure a satisfactory therapeutic result.

6. Periodic Paralysis

Mr. Wu, a 56-year-old farmer came to the hospital on 26 October 1989 with the chief complain of paralysis in the lower limbs for several days. There was nothing special in the past history and family history. He denied to have a trauma.

Examination revealed both lower limbs were in a state of

symmetrical paralysis. There was apparent weakened tendon reflex in the lower limbs. Serum potassium: 2. 8 mEq/liter; ECG: hypokalemia. The patient was diagnosed as periodic paralysis, and then he was treated with oral medicine and intravenous drip to supply potassium. He was transferred to Acupuncture Department next morning because of no improvement observed. After the needling on Dingzhongxian and Dingnie Qianxiexian (both sides) with the method of "qi withdrawal", the patient could stand up and walk a little immediately, and then he was able going home which was about 100 meters away from the hospital. On his way back home, he fell once but stood up again and walked home all by himself. Next morning the patient felt much improvement in the strength of his lower limbs and was completely cured after seven treatments.

Note: This is a typical periodic paralysis of both lower limbs. The scalp needling was very effective. Only after two treatments the patient was cured nearly completely. There was no relapse in the recent follow-up.

7. Poliomyelitis

Ye, an infant of 4 months visited on 21 June 1989, had a sudden high fever on 28 May 1989 and a paralysed weakness in his left lower limb was observed the next morning. The patient was taken to the Acupuncture Department then. The doctor was told that he had taken a poliomyelitis oral vaccine the night before he was found feverish.

Examination revealed that the mentality of the patient was clear with no fever. The left lower limb was weak and the skin temperature was colder than that of the right. There was also no tendon reflex. The baby was diagnosed as poliomyelitis. Acupuncture was carried out in the following points: Huantiao (GB 30), Biguan (ST 31), Fengshi (GB 31), Futu (ST 32), Zusanli (ST 36), Yanglingquan (GB 34), Xuanzhong (GB 39) and Jiexi (ST 41). A shallow needling was performed and the needle was withdrawn right after 2 to 3 twirling and rotating.

The treatment was given once daily for a total 10 treatments as a course.

After the first therapeutic course, the temperature began to rise in the affected limb and the movement was improved. After a rest for 5 days, the baby began to receive the second course, during which the treatment was given once every other day. Like this, altogether 4 therapeutic courses were performed, and the spacing between two courses varied from 10 to 30 days. The patient was then nearly completely cured. There was no muscular atrophy. in early 1990, the parents took the baby to the hospital again because they found there was abnormal gait on the part of the baby. therefore another two therapeutic courses with electric needling were prescribed.

During the follow-up examination in 1991, it was found that the baby had normal myodynamia. There were no muscular atrophy, no deformity of the hip, knee and ankle joints. But there is still slight abnormal gait because of the weakness of bending and stretching in the toe joints.

Note: In treating this patients, points are mainly selected from the 3 Foot Yangming Yin Meridians. The shallow needling with slight twirling and rotating can eliminate the pathogenic factor of excess type. Later in order to avoid muscular atrophy and joint deformity, increased stimulation including the use of electrotherapy was performed. A satisfactory therapeutic effect was finally obtained.

8. Facial Paralysis

Mr. Lu, a 40 years old officer visited on 9 May 1991, complained of deviation of his eyes and mouth yesterday night.

Examination revealed disappearance of the right frontal cross striation, incomplete closure of the eyelids, shallowed nasolabial fold, deviation of the mouth corner to the left side and hypogeusesthesia of the right side. There was also air leakage when blowing and the food was often found remaining around the mouth. There were no pain or tenderness at anywhere and no symptoms of the central nervous system. The patient was diagnosed as peripheral facial paralysis. Then a No. 30 needle of 1. 5—3 cun long was selected for penetration-acupuncture from Yangbai (GB 14) to Yuyao (EX-HN 4), from Taiyang (KI 1) to Jiache (ST 6) and from Jiache (ST 6) to Dicang (ST 4). Meanwhile, Sibai (ST 2), Yifeng (SJ 7) and Hegu (LI 4) were needled. All the points except Hegu were taken from the affected side. A G-6805 stimulator was connected to the needles on Yangbai, Sibai, Taiyang and Jiache for 20 minutes with continuous wave. Mild stimulation was performed for the first five treatments, and strength of stimulation increased for the later five treatments. The electromagnetic irradiation was also added. The treatment was given once every other day. 10 treatments constitute one therapeutic course. The patient was completely cured after one therapeutic course with no sequela at all.

Note: The points were selected very properly in this case. When electrotherapy was used, the patient was cured completely. Therefore, it proves that the concept of "Acupuncture can not be applied during the acute stage of facial paralysis" is not correct.

9. Injury of the Ulnar Nerve

Mr. Li, a male clerk of 52 years old, visited on 16 May 1991, and complained of numbness in his ulnar muscles after a long trip on a bus.

Examination showed weakness in bending his left hand, muscular relax in the hypothenar, difficulty in moving the 4—5th finger joints with weakened superficial sensibility. The patient was diagnosed as injury of the ulnar nerve. Then acupuncture treatment was prescribed and the following points were selected: Xiaohai (SI 8), Shaohai (HT 3), Quchi (LI 11), Zhizheng (SI 7), Waiguan (SJ 5), and Houxi (SI 3). After deqi (arrival of qi) the needles were connected to a G-6805 stimulator for 20 minutes. The treatments were given once every other day. 10 treatments constitute one therapeutic course. The patients was cured after one course of treatment.

Note: The injury of the ulnar nerve in this case was caused by long compression. The symptoms were comparatively milder. Due to the early treatment and frequent massage on the affected part, the patient enjoyed a quick recovery.

10. Hysterical Paralysis

Mr. Wang, a 22-year-old farmer, visited on 26 July 1985, and complained of a sudden onset of weakness in both lower limbs while working in the fields about one hour before, and then paralysis set in completely. He was immediately taken to the hospital.

Examination revealed that the patient could not stand. Tendon reflex and myodynamia were both normal. There was no pathological reflex. He was diagnosed as hysterical paralysis. Yongquan (KI 1) on both sides were needled swiftly with a No. 26 needle of 1. 5 cun long. A strong stimulation was induced by lifting, thrusting, twirling and rotating. Then some jerks on the lower limbs were noticed. The needles were retained for 10 minutes, during which the needles were manipulated 3 times. After the needles were withdrawn, the patient was asked to get off the bed. Under the encouragement of the doctor, the patient could walk with increasingly stable steps. After a while, he was well again as before.

Note: This case had a sudden onset, but the patient received an immediate treatment. In the treatment, Yongquan was needled with strong stimulation. At the same time, the suggestion was applied to encourage the patient. The author had treated many cases by this method with satisfactory results.

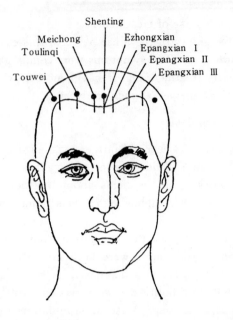

Fig. 5   Standard nomenclature of scalp acupoints (the front side)

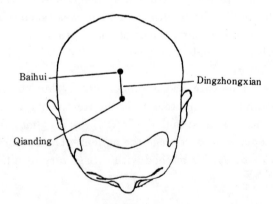

Fig. 6   Standard nomenclature of scalp acupoints (superior aspect)

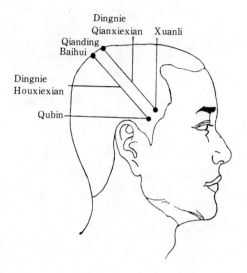

Fig. 7 Standard nomenclature of scalp acupoints (right lateral aspect)

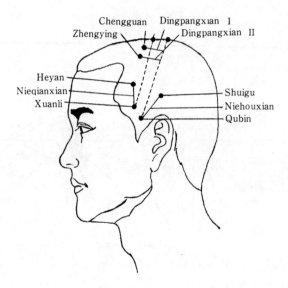

Fig. 8 Standard nomenclature of scalp acupoints (left lateral aspect)

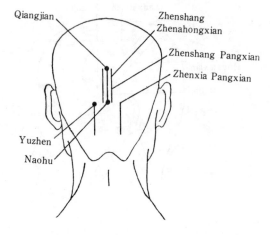

Fig. 9　Standard nomenclature of scalp acupoints (the back side)

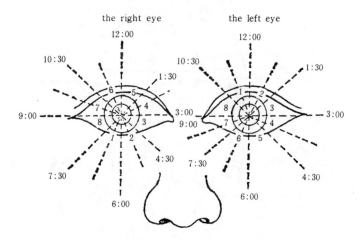

Fig. 10　The distribution of the points around the eyes

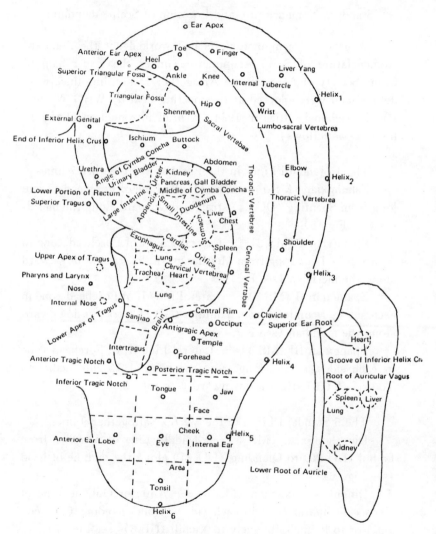

Fig. 11   Schematic diagram of distribution of auricular points

APPENDIX I

Standard Nomenclature and Location of Scalp Acupoints

A group of acupunctureists had worked out the Standard Nomenclature of Scalp Acupuncture under the leadershaip of China Society of Acupuncture Altogether 14 needling lines were defined and were adopted at the meeting held by WHO Westem Pacific Regional Office in 1984. A brief introduction of the 14 lines are as follows:

The 4 Standard Lines in the Forehead (altogether 7 limes)

Ezhongxian (MS 1)——the Middle Line of Forehead: 1 cun long from Shenting (DU 24) straight downward along the meridian (see Fig, 5)

Epangxian I (MS 2)——Lateral Line I of Forehead (one in each side): 1 cun long from Meichong (BL 3) straight downward along the meridian (see Fig, 5)

Epangxian II (MS 3)——Lateral Line II of Forehead (one in each side): 1 cun long from Toulinqi (GB 41) straight downward along the meridian (see Fig. 5)

Epangxian III (MS 4)——Lateral Line III of Forehead (one in each side): 1 cun long from the point 0. 75 cun medial to Touwei (ST 8) straight downward (see Fig. 5)

The 5 Standard Lines in the Vertex (altogether 9 lines)

Dingzhongxian (MS 5)—— Middle Line of Vertex: from Baihui (DU 20) to Qianding (DU 21) along the midline of head (see Fig. 6)

Dingnie Qianxiexian (MS 6)——Anterior Oblique Line of Vertex-Temporal (one in each side): from Qianding (1. 5 cun anterior to Baihui) obliquely to Xuanli (GB 6) (see Fig. 7)

Dingnie Houxiexian (MS 7)——Posterior Oblique Line of Vertex-Temporal (one in each side): from Baihui (DU 20) obliquely to Qubin (GB 7) (see Fig. 7)

Dingpangxian I (MS 8)——Lateral Line 1 of Vertex (one in each side): 1 cun long lateral to Middle Line of Vertex, 2 cun long from Chengguang (BL 6) backward along the meridian (see Fig. 8)

Dingpangxian II (MS 9)——Lateral Line 2 of Vertex (one in each side): 2.25 cun lateral to middle line of vertex, 1.5 cun long from Zhengying (GB 17) backward along the meridian (see Fig. 8)

The 2 Standard Lines in Temporal Area (altogether 4 lines)

Nieqianxian (MS 10)——Anterior Temporal Line (one in each side): from Hanyan (GB 4) to Xuanli (GB 6)(see Fig. 8)

Niehouxian (MS 11): Posterior Tempral Line (one in each side): from Shuaigu (GB 8) to Qubin (GB 7)(see Fig. 8)

The 3 Standard Lines in Occiput Area (altogether 5 lines)

Zhenshang Zhengzhongxian (MS 12)—— Upper-Middle Line of Occiput: from Qiangjian (DU 18) to Naohu (DU 17)(see Fig. 9)

Zhenshang Pangxian (MS 13)—— Upper-Lateral Line of Occiput (one in each side): 0.5 cun lateral and parallel to Upper-Middle Line of Occiput (see Fig. 9)

Zhenxia Pangxian (MS 14)——Lower-Lateral Line of Occiput (one in each side): 2 cun long from Yuzhen (BL 9) straight downward (see Fig. 9)

APPENDIX II

Acupoints Around the Eye Orbit

The Eye acupuncture was put forward by Prof. Peng Jing-shan from Liaoning College of Traditional Chinese Medicine a few years ago. As all the points are located around the eyeball and around the eye orbit, and the points must be identified according to the color changes of the blood vessels in bulbar conjunctiva, it is known as Eye Acupuncture, and the points are called "points around the orbit". The points can be taken in the following method.

The eye is divided into four quadrants by a horizontal line which goes through the center of the pupil and extends through the inner-outer canthus and a vertical line which also goes through the center of the pupil and extends through the upper-lower orbits. Then each quadrant is divided again into 2 equal areas (that is, 4 quadrants and 8 areas). These eight equal areas are actually eight point areas. (see Fig. 10)

Area 1 represents the Lungs and Large Intestine

Area 2 represents the Kidney and Bladder

Area 3 represents the Upper-Jiao

Area 4 represents the Liver and Gallbladder

Area 5 represents the Middle-Jiao

Area 6 represents the Heart and Small Intestine

Area 7 represents the Spleen and Stomach

Area 8 represents the Lower-Jiao

The orientation for each area can be demonstrated with a clock. Each area occupies 90 minutes. For the left eye, take it clockwise. For example, the Area 1 of the left eye is located between 10 ∶ 30 to 12 ∶ 00. For the right eye, take it in counterclockwise direction. For example, Area 1 of the right eye located from 7 ∶ 30 to 06 ∶ 00.

In the eight areas, there are altogether 13 points. In each of Area 1, 2, 4, 6, 7, there are one Zang organ and one Fu organ sharing it. For Area 3,5 and 8, it is occupied by the Upper, Middle and Lower Jiao respectively.

The points are all located around the eyeball and orbit, about the width of a finger away from the eyeball. The upper orbit is from the lower edge of the eyebrow and the lower orbit is about 0.2 cun from the edge of the eye orbit.

There are three methods to locate the points.

1. Press lightly with even force across the point area with a dappen stick or the handle of a three-edged needle. If a sensation of soreness, numbness, distension, heaviness or warmth, coolness, slight pain or comfort was experienced by the patient, here is a point. If there is nothing felt by the patient, press lightly the area. The spot where there is a small pit can be taken as a point.

2. Find the points with a Jingluo determinator. When the probe is used to press the area, we can determine the point by reading the meter. Usually the reading on a point is the largest.

3. In the selected point area, first determine exactly its limit and then perform perpendicular needling or lblique needling along the skin.

APPENDIX III

Standard Nomenclature and Location of Ear Acupoints (Fig. 11)

Middel Ear (Diaphragm): Helix crus.

Lower Portion of Rectum: On the end of helix approximate to superior tragic notch.

Urethra: On helix at level with the lower border of inferior antihelix crus.

External Genitalia: On helix at level with the upper border of inferior antihelix crus.

Front Ear Apex (Hemarrhoidal Nucleus): Area between ear apex and superior root of auricle.

Ear Apex: At the tip of auricle and superior to helix when folded towards tragus.

Liver Yang: At auricular tubercle.

Helix 1—6: Region from lower border of auricular tubercle to midpoint of lower border of lobule is divided into five equal parts. The points marking the divisions are respectively Helix 1, Helix 2, Helix 3, Helix 4, Helix 5, Helix 6.

Finger: At the top of scapha.

Interior Tubercle (Urticaria or Allergic Point): Midpoint between Finger and Wrist.

Wrist: Midway between Elbow and Finger.

Elbow: Midway between Finger and Clavicle.

Shoulder: Midway between Elbow and Clavicle.

Clavicle: On scapha at level with helix-tragic notch.

Toe: Superior and lateral angle of superior antihelix crus.

Heel: Superior and medial angle of superior of antihelix crus.

Ankle: Midway between heel and knee.

Knee: Middle portion at superior antihelix crus.

Hip: At inferior 1/3 of the superior antihelix crus.

Buttocks: At lateral 1/3 of the inferior antihelix crus.

Ischium (Sciatic Nerve): At medial 2/3 of the inferior antihelix crus.

End of Inferior Antihelix crus (Sympathetic Nerve): The terminal of inferior antihelix crus.

Cervical Vertebrae, Thoracic Vertebrae, Sacral Vertebrae: A curved line from helixtragic notch to the branching area of superior and inferior antihelix crus can be divided into 3 equal segments. The lower 1/3 of it is Cervical Vertebrae, the middle 1/3 is Thoracic Vertebrae, and the upper 1/3 is Lumbosacral Vertebrae.

Neck: On the border of cavum conchae of Cervical Vertebrae.

Chest: On the border of cavum conchae of Thoracic Vertebrae.

Abdomen: On the border of cavum conchae of Lumbosacral Vertebrae.

Ear-Shenmen: At bifurcating point between superior and inferior antihelix crus, and at the lateral 1/3 of triangular fossa.

Triangular Depression (Tiankui Uterus Seminal Palace): In the triangular fossa and in the depression close to the midpoint of helix.

Superior Triangle (Lowering Blood Pressure): At the superior-lateral angle of Triangular Fossa.

Superior Tragus (Ear): On the supratragic notch close to helix.

Nose (External Nose): In the centre of lateral aspect of tragus.

Supratragic Apex (Tragic Apex): At the tip of upper protuberance on border of tragus.

Infratragic Apex (Adrenal): At the tip of lower tubercle on border of tragus.

Pharynx-Larynx: Upper half of medial aspect of tragus.

Internal Nose: Lower half of medial aspect of tragus.

Antitragic Apex (Soothing Asthma or Parotid): At the tip of antitragic.

Middle Border (Brain): Midpoint between antitragic apex

and helix-tragic notch.

Occiput: At posterior superior corner of lateral aspect of antitragus.

Temple (Taiyang): On antitragus between Forehead and Occiput.

Forehead: At anterior inferior corner of lateral aspect of antitragus.

Brain (Subcortex):

Mouth: Close to posterior and superior border of orifice of external auditory meatus.

Esophagus: At medial 2/3 of inferior aspect of helix crus.

Cardiac Orifice: At area where helix crus terminates.

Duodenum: At lateral 1/3 of superior aspect of helix crus.

Small Intestine: At middle 1/3 of superior aspect of helix crus.

Appendix: Between Small Intestine and Large Intestine.

Large Intestien: At medial 1/3 of superior aspect of helix crus.

Liver: At posterior aspect of Stomach and Duodenum.

Pancrease: Between Liver and Kidney.

Kidney: On the lower border of inferior antihelix crus, directly above Small Intestine.

Ureter: Between Kidney and Bladder.

Bladder: On the lower border of inferior antihelix crus, directly above Large Intestine.

Angle of Cymba Conchae: At medial superior angle of Cymba.

Middle Cymba Conchae (Periphery Umbilicus): In the certer of Cymba Conchae.

Heart: In the central depression of cavum conchae.

Lung: Aroung Heart.

Trachea: In the area of Lung, between Mouth and Heart.

Spleen: Inferior to Liver, at lateral and superior aspect of cavum conchae.

Sanjiao: Superior to Intertragus.

Intertragus (Endocrine): At the base of cavum conchae in the intertragic notch.

Frontal Tragic Notch (Eye 1): On lateral and anterior side of intertragic notch.

Lower Tragic Notch (Elevating Blood Pressure Point): On the inferior aspect of intertragic notch.

Back Tragic Notch (Eye 2): On lateral and inferior aspect of intertragic notch.

Cheek: On the ear lobe, at posterior and superior aspect of Eye.

Tongue: In the centre of 2nd section of lobule.

Jaw: In the centre of 3rd section of lobule.

Section 4 of Ear Lobe (Neurasthenic Point): In the 4th section of ear lobe.

Eye: In the 5th section of ear lobe.

Internal Ear: In the 6th section of the ear lobe.

Tonsil: In the 8th section of the ear lobe.

Upper Root of Auricle (Middle Stasis or Spinal Cord): At the upper border of the auricular root.

Lower Root of Auricule: On the lower border of the juncture between the ear lobe and the cheek.

Root of Auricular Vagus Nerve: At the junction of retroauricle and mastoid, level with helix crus.

Groove of Inferior Helix Crus (Groove for Lowering Blood Pressure): Through the backside of superior antihelix crus and inferior antihelix crus, in the depression as a "Y" form.

Heart: At the upper back of the ear.

Spleen: In the middle at the back of the ear.

Liver: On the back of ear, at lateral aspect of Spleen.

Lung: On the back of the ear, at medial aspect of Spleen.

Kidney: At the lower part of the retroauricle.

INDEX FOR DISEASES